A HUNTER'S LIFE LIVED

A Hunter's Life Lived

Copyright © 2020 by Michael Hunte. All rights reserved.

No part of this publication may be reproduced, stored in a retrieval system, or transmitted in any form or by any means, digital, electronic, mechanical, photocopying, recording, or otherwise, or conveyed via the Internet or a website without prior written permission of the publisher, except in the case of brief quotations embodied in critical articles and reviews.

ISBN: 978-1-7358263-0-1

Cover photo taken by *Peter W. Goff* in 1968

Printed in the United States of America

A HUNTER'S LIFE LIVED

Remastered by Caroline Lester

MICHAEL HUNTE

1

(This page to be entirely free from erasure)

Description of Soldier on leaving Army Service

Year of Birth 24-1-41   Height 5 ft. 9 ins.
Complexion COLOURED   Eyes D/BROWN   Hair BLACK
Marks and Scars (Visible) Op Scar   Blood Group ....
Rt Neck

Assessments of Military Conduct and Character

Military Conduct VERY GOOD

Note—The Range of Military Conduct Gradings possible is:—
(1) Exemplary (available only to men with a minimum of 6 years' service)
(2) Very Good (3) Good (4) Fair (5) Unsatisfactory

Testimonial. (*To be completed with a view to civil employment*)

Hunte is a thoroughly reliable, good natured and hard working man. He has served in the Regiment as a cook and has shown great skill both in the field and in barracks. He is particularly good at overcoming difficulties by using his powers of improvisation and initiative. He has a zest for life and sense of humour that are extremely refreshing. His conduct during army service has been very good.

The above assessments have been read to me.
Signature of Soldier ....

Place ALDERSHOT

(Signature of C.O.)

Date 31 Oct. 1966

Unit 1 PARACHUTE REGIMENT RHA

TABLE OF CONTENTS

Chapter 1	I Am Island Born	1
Chapter 2	My Aunt Doots, a Wise Woman	9
Chapter 3	Wanting a Slice of the Empire's "Cake"	13
Chapter 4	Hunter On Schooling	17
Chapter 5	The Mother Country Calls	21
Chapter 6	A Family of Women	25
Chapter 7	In Human Nature	27
Chapter 8	What's in a Name?	31
Chapter 9	Alone Without Laws	35
Chapter 10	The Chattel Houses	41
Chapter 11	The After Years	45
Chapter 12	High Winds Blow Over Barbados	47
Chapter 13	The Memories of Growing Up	51
Chapter 14	Clear Blue Seawater	53
Chapter 15	The Long Road	57
Chapter 16	A Sort of Word Blindness	61
Chapter 17	I Believe in Them	65
Chapter 18	Skin Color as the Status	69
Chapter 19	Healthy Genes Have Been Given	71
Chapter 20	Learning to Fly	75
Chapter 21	I Am Proud To Be One	79
Chapter 22	The Fallout of Nuclear	81
Chapter 23	Nuclear Fallout	83

Chapter 23	War Came Close. 87
Chapter 24	The Food Revolution 91
Chapter 25	A Dream Lived. 95
Chapter 26	The Computer Age Came. 97
Chapter 27	The Computer Came Home. 101
Chapter 28	Meeting My Father. 103
Chapter 29	My Father's Death 105
Chapter 30	A Chance Meeting 109
Chapter 31	Jazz a Language of Love 113
Chapter 32	Sugar and the Economy 125
Chapter 33	Hunte on Jury Service. 129
Chapter 34	An Invitation to an Imaginary Meeting. 133

CHAPTER 1

I AM ISLAND BORN

There was a celebration at my birth by the women in my life at that time—my mother, her mother, and her two sisters. It was the start of something big. Seventy-nine years after this baby boy made his entrance into the world, I am now heading for the status of an older man. I will say that I expect most of my life has been lived so far. Some of what I have experienced I would like to share with you.

I have lived above, probably surpassed my expectations of the mark I had given myself. I cannot speak for others and what they had me listed down as. I know hopes were high, with my being the first boy of that generation, so some, including myself, had hopes far beyond my reach. Education on the island when I attended school was inferior. Bad, I might have said. That was before when I was young and angry. I now see no reason why I cannot repeat it if it comes into my thoughts. The method of teaching was terrible; I can say that with authority because I was there. I suffered at the hands of the teachers. I know I said it before, but I think it's worth mentioning again so that, if you're reading this, you understand. I'm saying how much it's hurting me. I'm nearly eighty years old and I'm speaking of what happened when I was ten or eleven years old.

A baby boy is born into a house of joy, a two-bedroom wooden apartment, with shingle roof and bedrooms separated by printed cotton curtains blowing in the wind. I saw it as a forerunner for the flat pack houses because they could be moved on, taken to a new location. Sunday was the best day to relocate to a new rented plot of land.

Men would start to gather at about 6:30 a.m. They came one by one with ropes and many nails. The land would be rented, so if you found a better plot of land, you would apply for it, and you would move your house onto it. The men would arrive early morning on a Sunday, by which time we would have packed up everything in bundles and placed outside. Most of the cooking utensils were boxed up or put to one side, except those being used, because lunch would be prepared for the workers.

By 5:00 p.m., when the hot sun had lost its heat and was setting, it was time to move back into the house. The first night was always rough, as it is for any move to a new location. The cast iron bed would be first to get assembled, the head and a foot part, then two sides fitted in, coil springs in place and a mattress on top. One after another, these beds were assembled. The house furniture followed, the whatnot, dining room table and chairs, and the dry goods into the larder. As far as I can remember, the small box ladder stood on four legs. Each leg was a saucer with water as to stop the ants. All four legs stood in a saucer fill with water in to stop the ants crawling, up the legs and entering the food ladder. Today, most houses have fridges and water toilets. Refrigerators were not standard then, but we had iceboxes. We could buy the ice and put it in the box, and it would keep your food fit for eating for a few days. By Sunday night, the workers and helpers would slowly drift away. The truck has long gone after delivering the central part of the wooden frame and sides. As demand for lifters and shifters started to drift off, before they went, a bottle of rum would be passed around. There were toasts and good wishes for the stay in the house and then they'd be gone.

Back then, in January 1941, the world war was taking place. The Europeans were fighting and killing each other. For the land and its riches, they had stolen from its rightful owners.

First, they stole the people and what was in the field. It was the destruction of both buildings and people and their ancestry, all for greed. At home and on others' land, this killing took place and involved others who had no say in it. A trial run for this war started back in 1914 due to a misunderstanding of the poor and their needs. It had slowed down when the shooting stopped. That war ended in 1918. Then twenty years later, it was war as usual. This time it would involve more men, women, and children. The rich and the poor would take their place in the fight, albeit for power, possession of land, or just being servile.

It moved from the battlefields to the Bier Keller's in Germany, at a time when the Deutschmark was taking a hammering in the money marketplace. A boy started the First World War; he killed a duke and his wife. As I read this, it reads like fiction, something I have read and put away, but it is a fact. It was a sick teenager who kick-started the First World War.

With added music, this has overtures of *Oedipus Rex*, without the sex, a great tragedy in the making. Looking at it now, that was just the beginning. One, the world would be drawn like no other of tyranny; it spread all over the world. He was sick and probably dying a slow death. Mad with his illness and the society he was living in, he thought he would do something about it.

The world was a vastly different place then. Corrupt men ran the world, some with stupidity and the rest with jealousy. The British Empire was at its highest. I was born into a world of trouble, big trouble. However, the boy grew up to be a fine strapping and fearless young man. I am writing about myself as I head for old age and retirement, about life I have lived and am living now. I am now older and a bit wiser, full of memories that I have lived and tales to tell of what I packed into my younger years. I have recorded my life in my own words with some input from a few friends. As you may or may not know, for those who don't, the English language is alive and growing daily. New words pop into literature and some dropout. The word *nigger* dropped out. When it was used, I don't think those who used it meant it as derogatory. The writers of that time used it to their advantage. The world was young, and being young, it was exciting to explore and steal. All who conquer take from those they have conquered.

From the verbal information I have gathered about my birth as I was growing up, it was a day to remember. My arrival was anticipated by a few mothers, not just my mother, who was giving birth to her firstborn. It was a joyful time; it would have been a time to say, "Let's have a drink and pour the rum." Poor man, a boy is born, and rum has a very distinctive smell that comes from caramels and the aroma of spices. As a boy growing up on the inland when the croups of sugar were ready, soon one would smell the boiling of the juices that would become sugar. One can feel it in the air for miles as the wind takes across the inland. The bell plantation was close to where I live at that time of growing up.

My mother was the youngest of three daughters, born to Florence Hunte, my grandmother. Violet, her youngest daughter, gave birth to me on January 24, 1941. Her two older sisters, my aunts Pearl and Audrey, were both in attendance. This was taking place in a two-room wooden chattel house, the same type of home that the slaves would have lived in.

The house was made of lumber probably shipped across the Atlantic from Canada. With its vast amount of timber, it was the right place to supply all the lumber needed for the building of cheap housing, the same as was for the slavers. All that was required for the building would have come either from the USA or Canada. The wood or lumber, as it was called, the bolts and nails, this type of housing was a forerunner for the now-well-known flat pack. The floor laid down. First, the four sides slid into place and bolted together. The plot of land rented from the estate, so the family could take the house and fit it up elsewhere.

The chattel wooden houses were poorly designed for the weather the island had to endure; they had not changed all that much by the time I was born. Some are still in use today. Some of them in use today have an added front part of the house made with beech block. The house I was born in is still standing and occupied, not at the same address. We lived in Goddard's Road, Carrington Village in the parish of St. Michael, Barbados, West Indies.

At my birth, there were lots of excitement in the household; a boy has now been added to the family of five women. Having a new birth meant there had to be a "man in the mix," at the point of conception at least. None seemed to stay around. That was how it was handed down from slavery, what I call breeding to keep up the stock after the trade was outlawed. I was born 168 years after the abolition of slavery. The plantation relied 100 percent on labor, and I'll say 95 percent came from black men and women.

The stupid men who sat in London's House of Commons—well, I might be using the word in haste, but let us look at the facts at the time of the passing of the act—would have been slave owners. So ebbing a few more years out of the hard-working slavers would have worked for them. The act declares that before the enslaved men, women, and children became free. Some of the MP sitting in the House of Commons deliberately went against the ruling, saying that the slavers should learn to be a slave by serving a period of apprenticeship, doing work they were doing all their lives, before they received full emancipation as many women and children.

This was after they did the job, whatever it was, they had grown into it, some from birth and was added as stocked.

It was so the owners' vote to squeeze another few more working years out of hard-working years out of the enslaved. Men, women, and children—their freedom was granted to them in 1834 by the houses of Parliament in London.

I can say with conviction that those men in their blonde wigs, sitting in their posh seats, never knew of or saw the conditions the slaves lived and worked in. Once you are in power, it's my belief, it has a profound effect on those who have the ability. It can have a lasting hypnotic impact on the one being picked on, a feeling as the outsider, which can last forever. When it goes, it can and will leave you naked to the world, just like the school's playground bully who picks on another boy or girl and is encouraged by others. As he is praised and geared on by others but him or her on their own can revert to being shy, lacking confidence, a shy young introvert. Yes, it was rough, and it is going to be so. They did not have to serve time learning to be slaves. They were in at the deep end from day one.

The men in London, and they were all men, had no idea of what life was like living and working there. What would they have had? A few drawings and descriptions.

This was the trend introduced by slave owners, to produce its own from the stock already on the plantation, "homegrown" slaves bred from cradle to field. For me, I had the privilege of home birth with one midwife in attendance. There were lots of old woven cotton bags that once contained flour or rice from the USA used as towels. Plenty of hot water was needed, and lots of women were in attendance. They carried water from a standpipe in buckets and heated it on a fire, fueled by cane pith and pods from the mahogany tree. This type of light was still in use when I was growing up. The seed is shaped like avocado and about the same size. As a boy, I used to go and pick up the spent pods for firewood. Inside the pod, there were lots of seeds shaped like interval propeller blades that would have flown on the wind. Once they reached a specific temperature, they opened. We often sat and watched the seeds fly as we took shade from the hot sun before we made our way home, laden with the pods for firewood, me and cousin Ruby. It was a day or a few hours out at least, for us growing up. It's possible, it was the pod of the mahogany tree that Leonardo da Vinci saw spinning and floating down. Heading for the ground, as it opened, the pod released its offspring in seeds. With an added bit of imagination that Leonardo da Vinci would have had, it was as an engine flying. Lying under the tree in the midday sun, watching the seeds float to the ground so free. It needs to be seen to be understood, but take my word for it, as I sat watching day after day, watching the pods open and the insides take to the wind and float to the ground. The hefty bulbous tip would take root when rain and sun fell on it.

The British ruled their empire by a divide-and-conquer rule. I say that because drying food was never passed on. For instance, it was in India that the British learned to dry food.

In the Caribbean medley Barbados, there were plenty of fish, so you ate it. That was that. The same thing with pickled vegetables. Vegetables never came to us in plenty, so it was as the saying "boom or bust." In Africa, there is a pepper sauce called papa's pepper sauce. In Ghana, they have hot pepper sauce. It's a strange mixture of dried fish and peppers. Barbados has its hot pepper sauce, which is made from scotch bonnet peppers, shallot onions, a dash of molasses, and mustard.

CHAPTER 2

MY AUNT DOOTS, A WISE WOMAN

My aunt Doots had no schooling for she had to keep moving alongside her mother, my grandmother, the work was scarce, and they had to take what was available at the time: the cropping of sugarcane that would have been excellent for the temporary workers, both men and women. The work was backbreaking, but the pay was as good as it got for those times. I have read files about the work, so I feel I have experienced the pain that the job brought. The men cut the cane using a machete, and they aimed for the roots an inch or two above the lowest "eye"—these are joins or sections that appear on the cane. They then struck above the eye with a machete, holding the chain in one hand. Then with their free hand, they turned it, with a flip of the handheld machete—the more it is used and sharpened, the thinner it becomes.

The men would take off the top part and throw the green tops off, then cut it just above the roots. Some of the green tops were fed to the cows. When drinking their milk, one can taste the cane tops.

My grandmother and Aunt Doots took washing in or any general work whatever there was at the time, knocking on the houses and asking if any housework was needed. If the answer was no, They just moved on to the next house and so on day in and day out. The men had the upper hand when looking for work; they worked regularly and got what they demanded. And I would say, sex was not excluded, because in the days of slavery, they were encouraged, so that would have been handed down to them. Though they were now free, they would have continued doing the same as before.

I was never adopted, but she, my aunt Doots, she was the one for me, for it was her I ran to. It was she who anointed me with oils and words of confidence with her smooth words. She made tea from a bush that grew by the roadside. A bottle of seawater used to hang outside her back door, which also served as a medicine. I still take some when I am on the island. When I take a sea bath, I cup my hands and scoop some water and drink it. I had swallowed the seawater from the Atlantic, Arabian Gulf, and the Indian Ocean when I was in Kenya. Does that method work? I don't know if it works for everyone, but it certainly works for me.

Because when the slaves arrived, they had no medicine apart from seawater. They would have been washed down on the ship, scooping up seawater and would have washed down the decks. That must have been a terrible stench, but a trusted slave, a deckhand, would be given that job, probably before breakfast. A change from the seat they had sat on for almost three weeks' journey across the Atlantic.

Back to my aunt Doots, she was the wise one, no schooling that I know of, and she was uneducated, I believe. Yet still, she knew I found it hard to comprehend others at times, with her insight. The eldest of three daughters, she would have seen, felt, and experienced the hardship she and her mother had to endure like many others at the time she was born out of wedlock. I wonder if you can understand that it could be difficult if you had a good upbringing. After the end of the slave trade, no more young men and women could be imported from Africa. So having humiliated the men and women by capture into slavery, they lost their names, way of life, and whatever else was taken away from them. This is how the slave owners started their breeding farm.

The island is a portion of land initially surrounded by water, 366 square miles of coral reef area on the island of Barbados. The first slave code was to introduced on the island; it was a very violent practice carried out by the slave owners. They would boil a man in a vat of hot sugar as an example to others who felt rebellious. The years rolled on, and money invested the return profitable in a short time. Lots of grand houses were built in Britain off the backs of slave labor. One thing that is not obvious to many, slavery gave us the train, not for passengers to get from A to B, but for the project to reach its report back to England. Anyone with limited imagination could see why others got jealous and wanted some of the same.

CHAPTER 3

WANTING A SLICE OF THE EMPIRE'S "CAKE"

The cake was so rich and there was so much of it. In other words, there was enough to go around, but greed played a big part in it.

The Second World War had been going for two years. I will expand on this later in a timeline. In January 1941, the year I was born, it unfolded that one mad man got the war started in Europe. This time it would stretch across the globe.

I was raised from birth by my mother until I was about ten years old. Then she moved away to start a new life, with no room for me, so I lived in the family home. She married and moved away to begin her life as a married woman. I was an embarrassment to her as she had been an unmarried mother. It was an imitation of what was going in the UK.

I remember my grandmother would sit by the window in the evenings, looking out and watching the people walk by. The sunset gave light to another land. She'd watch the lamp flies lighting up their path, as they sought out food and played until dawn. The next morning, "Ma'am" as I called her, would get up, boil some water on the open fire, and make tea before she went off to work in the fields to weed or harvest whatever the crop was at the time.

At Christmastime, when I was a boy, the English society in Barbados, the owner of the house had a servant fetch sand from the beach. This would then be sprinkled around the house to emulate snow on the morning of December 25, Christmas Day. A day for the beach, I remember going for long walks, walking over the white sand, watching the water kissing the sand as the sandpipers running away as the wave coming in and deposited small crustaceans and runback as the tides resided.

Christmas on the island is emulated in the island to that of the English society, not that of Africa. It was as if slavery had not happened, that is what we were taught, no history as to why we inhabited the small island. It was a sort of embarrassment to the establishment, the books all written and printed in England. Probably giving a false picture of what England was like, small red brick cottages with thatched rooves, as seen on Christmas cards.

I lived in my grandmother's house, along with her daughter Ruby and Aunt Pearl, all women. The house was tiny, but somehow, we managed not to get in each other's way. It had clean wooden floors, scrubbed to an extremely high standard. We also used the outside yard as a room, cooking and washing were all done outside. The mornings and evenings were the best time to work, out when cooler. Weeding and tending to the few animals, fowl, and plants were all morning jobs along with the watering.

I do remember that the pillows on our beds were filled with cuscus grass. This emits a fragrance that is very relaxing and is still used today in modern perfumes. The mattresses were also stuffed with the green and, therefore, had to be shaken every morning. After a few months, we had to replenish the grass inside the bed mattresses, as the dried herb broke up and became too flat for comfort. During the first days of a refilled mattress, we slept in exceedingly high beds! So my fate was sealed, the die was cast, for me to be among women. I had another aunt who was married and lived about a mile and a half away from the family home. Her name was Aunt Audrey; to me, she was always Aunt Doots.

I did not have any male role models at home. I was like a son to her. Aunt Doots was a brave woman. She could not read or write, but she had a sense, an instinct. I would run to her for everything, even from a beating at school on one occasion. She was the only one who would listen to me, this barren woman. In her mind, she had adopted me. My mother had moved away from the family home. She started to build her new life, as mentioned earlier, leaving me with my elderly aunts once my grandmother had died. I was alone with no restrictions and no boundaries. I went feral; I got the feeling one was more reliable in a pack. I felt the stronger one is the less likely one was to be attacked when in a group. After a day at school, I ran with the pack of what I now know were wild boys. I ran around with some older boys until late at night. This pack of boys always dressed smartly. This was where I had my first look at blue jeans, like the ones the cowboys wore. Today, I can still be seen in a pair, and the copper rivets are missing, all that sitting by the campfire, the metal got hot and threatened to burn their manhood! So the makers removed them.

These were the wild boys older than myself. One was from my school, and he was the one who got me in the pack. They were the smartly dressed set, in the latest kit money could buy. To this day, I still wear the same jeans as I did then, over sixty years ago. They are cheaper than the others sold with big names on.

Aunt Pearl worked as a house servant for a family with a Welsh name I'm told. They lived in Belmont Road. After school, I would go to her place of work and help her finish off things like cleaning the gutters and sweeping the yard. We would then eat any food that was left when it came back from the family's table: a white family, part of the indenture men and women that came from Wales. Aunt Pearl worked as a general dogs body for the family—husband, wife, and their two sons.

Hundreds of such men and women were a product of what later became the British Empire. Whether voluntary or indentured, from Wales or Bristol, they had been taken to Barbados in the seventeenth or eighteenth century. Wales was a significant supplier of tools to the slave trade as was nearby Bristol. They made the chains that tethered the slave men and women to the seats for their journey across the Atlantic. This trade, these men and women of Wales who worked in a blacksmith, in my opinion, they saw no harm in making chains; they did not know what use their goods would have.

CHAPTER 4

HUNTER ON SCHOOLING

The education system, for some, was inferior. On reflection, it was close to being barbaric. That is my opinion. I am entitled to that. I was not someone looking in; I was in the storm of it all. I was almost eight years. I bear the scars today, and no one paid any attention to what was going on, so it went on year after year. I am entitled to speak of it because I lived through it.

This was the 1940s. More barbarism and pointless killings were going on in Europe. What we humans do to each other must be laughed at by other animals. Unnecessary killing of each other, and for what? For power, breeding rights, and dominion over others. Is it a rational reason to kill someone because someone in authority says so? I should know. I would ask that same question when Europeans arrived in Africa. The men and women were going about their daily business, but if they did not look like you, did not sound like you, the judgment was carried out, as they concluded that they were lesser humans if humans at all! To show their superiority, they took these Africans and made them work for them. They put them in chains and made them work, preparing and ploughing the land, ready for planting. They started with cotton and food, as the weather was good for this.

So the Atlantic slave trade began and not for the first time because the Arabs also took slaves from Africa. Some young men and women were up as capital for a loan. Like a pawnshop, a pledge on some piece of art or jewelry. If the bearer of the goods cannot pay, the young man or woman would be kept instead.

Some of those slaves did manage to return to their home after years of working, but let's put it this way, my ancestors did not make the trip. Yet in 1820, some freed slaves did make the trip back to Africa as free slaves. The British government in 1787 settled three hundred former slaves and a few white "women of the night" in Sierra Leone. However, three hundred out of thousands is no more than a drop in the ocean. What is clear is that the slave owners were not going to give up the workers' life and leave himself high and dry when there were crops to tend to and be harvested and taken to market.

I spent two years in Bahrain. My years there were from 1962 to 1963. It must have been extraordinary to see a black man in a white soldier's kit. I was approached by a group of young men. One of the workers was speaking in Arabic. All I could do was throw my hands up in the air, saying, "I don't understand." They wanted to know where I came from. I tried to point out a tiny island in the Caribbean, but to no avail. The Caribbean is not one mass of land as some think of it; it's a group of islands. With their governments, some are members of the United Nations. Small as they are, they have a vote in the assembly along with China, the USA, Russia, and a few more.

As I was carrying out my homework for this book, I found things out that I could never have done using legwork. For the record, I think I have mentioned it already so that I won't repeat it; I attended

St. Giles Boys School in Ivy Road. I later discovered that both St. Giles Boys School and the girl's school were built in 1819 on what is called free land. The two schools are close to each other, parted by a road. A wealthy sugar planter gave the money to purchase a plot of land and build a school. The ground was free for the poor. The school still stands today. When I attended the school way back in the 1940s, the headmaster was Mr. Cumberbatch who lived along Ivy Road. The teaching was good, but there was a state of madness going through the school, probably borrowed from the English. I use the word *lunacy*. I was beaten severely, with a few other boys who suffered the same fate as I did. Today, the scars are still on my hands, or maybe, they're imaginary. The strap used just to overreach the palm of my hand and land on my wrist because I could not spell or do mental arithmetic.

They are a lot of history that is missing when independence was granted to the people of Barbados in 1966. Some of the papers that are missing were shipped back to Britain. I would not say *stolen*, just they are ours. Burial documents back to England that means if a Bajan student is studying the life and time of the people, leaving the local historians wondering, what they cannot find these documents. Missing as well is the church record of birth and death. It's wartime tasted, destroy what we don't need, so they don't get to use it again.

Now I am not saying this is or was deliberate. Still, when the French departed from Algeria, a train moves along the tracks, breaking the sleepers back to Marseille. I am not saying that was their intension

CHAPTER 5

THE MOTHER COUNTRY CALLS

It took a war or two for the call to come for help, as the enemy was planning an invasion to take the empire the British had built up over the years. Lots of young men and women answered the call and were willing to put their lives on the line.

For freedom, the older women collected money to support the war fund. The island had been involved with war before my birth. The young men had fought for the "mother country" during the First World War too. It had left its mark on the men; it took time to adjust back to the healthy ways of island life. It was complicated.

The black soldiers complained about the duties they were given and the frequency of them. Their billet came around to clean the washroom and toilets more frequently than all the others in the camp. The black soldiers felt that they were picked on because they were black. Some refused to carry out their duties, saying they were the only ones to clean out the latrines. I can only imagine what happened to them. For the same thing happened to me when I was stationed in Bahrain in the 1960s, in what we called the Silver City. At the Hamala Camp, we were excused from cleaning the latrines, because our job was to work in the kitchen, preparing and cooking food.

One morning, a few new soldiers, who had come into the camp a few weeks ago, took it upon themselves to come into our hut talking. They were hard men. It can be seen from their billets. They seemed ready to fight. They said they never saw any of us from this hut cleaning the bog house and asked why not. The corporal in our hut put them right, by explaining why we were excused from cleaning toilet duties. We were involved in the preparation and cooking and serving food. That was reason enough. When it was put to them, it was accepted, and they walked away with the tails between their legs.

So I know the feelings around duties. A revolt was in the making. Some in the West Indies refused to work. The mutiny or revolt, as it was known, took place in Toronto in 1918.

The British West Indies Regiment was stationed in Toronto, being prepared for demobilization. They were required to carry out heavy duties, including building and cleaning latrines for the white soldiers. This caused resentment. It was tough to understand a court-martial during the time of war. With the facts at the time and the fear of fighting, men could be misunderstood. The soldiers felt they were severely treated. A court-martial was held. One soldier was found guilty and executed for his part in the mutiny. The court-martial took place in the last days of the war.

Men and women were asked to join and fight. War was raging in the Atlantic and the Caribbean seas. They were willing to risks their lives to cross the Atlantic to come and fight for Britain. From the start, they met racial prejudice on the ship crossing the Atlantic. Cold weather and rough seas in the Atlantic, forced the captain to take cover in Halifax, an eastern port in Canada. The officer in charge refused to issue the cold weather clothing. About half the men suffered from frostbite and the loss of limbs. They had to return to the Caribbean on their homes not having seen Europe or war, broken and disillusioned.

The history is still to be told of these brave men and women who put their lives on the line to protect others. Not much is written about these men and women; the years are getting for these men and women.

Volunteers played their roles in both world wars: The islanders were left on the own, with the odd overseer, those inhabitants who were injured under British rule. Barbados sent men and women off to fight. Some replied that it was not their fight. More has been written about pirates, fighting each other and the Spanish, killing and looting of the ships on the high seas. It was written as romance, for those thinking of faraway places. Yes, when the war came, the London war office sent out flyers, asking the men and women to go and fight for the mother country.

During the Second World War, merchant ships were lost to the bottom of the Atlantic. The German U-boats torpedoed them, sailing from the USA, Canada, and the Caribbean heading for the UK. They were laden with food, oil, and other much-needed materials, as well as crew to help the war effort. The German U-boats were patrolling the seas. I have a feeling that I saw one that made it to Barbados; I would have been about four years at the time. So far, my search on the Internet has not found it.

In 1941, it started to fall apart for the German high command. The war was mainly being fought in Europe and Africa. They had no political say in the fight, although many died as the bombs and bullets flew in their direction and on their land.

CHAPTER 6

A FAMILY OF WOMEN

Most families used to be made up of men and women; when I was born, there were only women in my family—the eldest being my grandmother, who never married, despite giving birth to three daughters, all by different fathers. By the time I came along, there were no men. I saw one or two hanging about. Myself and cousin Ruby gave one of them a nickname. He had a face with a pointed nose like that of a rodent, and we called him Rat Face.

As far as I can gather, during these troubled times, while the war was going on in Europe, the men had volunteered to fight. Women on the island were left to fend for themselves because most of the fit black men were away fighting in Europe.

Some of the women did what they had to do; the culture led to original work. Sometimes, they got the job done, whatever the job situation may be. This sort of thing happened, maybe in a job interview or a court case, the outcome could be based on accepting the terms of sexual favors or may result in rape. Slavery was over and laws been passed to end it, but some of its poisons lingered on in the power of the overseer. He who had the power hired and fired the workforce. With no one to complain to, they were often treated the same as the animals they looked after.

After the birth of her first child, my grandmother had to move on. It was hard scraping a living, for the women. In those days, there were still the memories of slavery, and that mindset lingered on long after. As women had no one to complain to, whatever their complaint, they had to deal with it themselves.

As the slaves had experienced, fear ruled their everyday lives. Do anything wrong and you would be beaten or killed as a warning example to others. It was a very turbulent and eventful time with revenge high on the list. You see, there was no need for the law when there was slavery. A slave owner had the right to do as he or she saw fit when it came to the treatment of their slaves. They were property owned by law. She or he had the right to kill a slave that was causing trouble. When murdering a slave was not a crime, so killing a slave was not reported, just that he or she was missing. There was no one to report it to. The plantation owner could always say that the slave had been sent to another property, and that was it, end of a conversation and no questions asked. Then came the end of owning slaves. Black women were not free. One could say it was a free for all, but they were not free. The now-free men and women emulated their ex-owners, by copying what they did and how they lived and once treated the slavers.

One can see how reprisal could be an issue for one-time owners. The now-free slaves emulated the lifestyle that their previous masters once had when they had been held captive. That was the blueprint of life and its standards. The Civil Code had to change, by that I mean the way you treated others. Not necessarily as some would wish to be treated—"Yes, sir, no, sir, three bags full, sir" and tip their hat to you.

CHAPTER 7

IN HUMAN NATURE

None of what you are reading is without fact; it may read like fiction to you at times if the truth was hidden away from you for reasons so as not to upset you. Then you could enjoy the fruits of other's labor, of those who were held and worked in bondage.

I have lived and experienced it. The little history I was taught when I attended school, was all about England. It would have been better if we had been told of how men and women were treated during slavery and after it ended.

For the black men and women who had gone over to fight and help keep Britain free, there was a sort of "thank you, now you can go home." I attended school in the late 1940s and early 1950s. The school had no books, no library, no gymnasium—well, it had nothing. The textbooks we used to read from were all written by English men and possibly women and printed in England. Come to think of it, those same books would probably have been sent off to Africa and India. Dare I say it, men who had never set sail to the colonies, living in London and parts of the British Isles, were also the men who wrote the history books?

In the forties, after the two world wars, guilt started to set in. It might have been my ignorance in how things worked, the prominent men in London who were calling the shots, had never set foot on the island, or if any did, they were very few. They paraded with Indian peacock feathers in their hats and their white suits with gleaming medals. That made them seem superior. Whereas in fact, they were just a heartbeat away from death like any of us. To make yourself look big in a battle or to be respected, the more significant your dress would be as in the North American Indians, who wore feathers on their heads to make them seem big and impressive? The Canadian black bear was used to supply the fur for the busby (worn by the queen's guards). In recent years, the busby is now made from nylon. There are five regiments in the British Army guardsmen: Grenadier Scots, Irish Welsh, and three Coldstream. These are regular soldiers who take their turn in frontline duties, not just dressed as toy soldiers in Whitehall, where people go to pose with them and see them in their colorful uniforms.

A soldier's job is not cut out to be just one thing; I'll say, his or her exercise is to look after the people of whom he is fighting to keep out of harm's way. Those of us who signed on the dotted line becomes the buffers representing and protecting the people of the nation of whom we approve of fighting. It is such a complicated job that there are a lot of days when nothing happened. Then all of a sudden, you're on your way to stand on fight, protecting, one day your boots of polish and gleaming you can see your face in them, on parade. You go through a ritual of getting ready for the parade—lots of spit and polish, uniform pressed. To get them like to hold the seen, we shave the inside of the trousers' legs. Metals polish if you have any of the right ribbons. My time in the army the battle dressed.

In Human Nature

My history is also of Great Britain, along with others who were born and bred in any of the lands that made up Great Britain's rule under the Union Jack. My family worked hard, day in and day out, under the flag of the Union Jack. My grandmother worked in the cane fields, which was backbreaking work, gathering the cane after the cutters let it drop to the ground. Then it was loaded onto trucks, and after that, it got sent along with cotton to the United Kingdom.

Let us all look at how this colossus mess got started, winners the takers and losers. We are all in it; one man changed the course of history for all of us.

In May 1625, young Captain John Powell sailed across the Atlantic and claimed the island of Barbados to be English on behalf of King James I. From then on, a lot of African men, women, and children's lives were ruined, stolen from their families and their countries. Their culture and family ties were lost forever, a way for the lives of others disregarded without question or a chance to plead. A lot of money was to be made for the perpetrators for the trade of kidnapping and selling men, women, and children. This was theft on a grand scale; no charges were brought, sailors coming ashore and making prisoners of them. I believe that until we can come to find peace, coinciding with other nations, we could end up having another world war. I am basing my belief on the Second World War, for the first one was supposed to be the war to end all wars. That was the line given to the young men before they went off to fight.

CHAPTER 8

WHAT'S IN A NAME?

I pose the question with meaning, for you may well have the name of your family that goes back centuries. You may well be able to trace it back to its roots. We, the offspring of slaves, just don't have that for, in the aftermath of slavery, ours were lost. Slaves lost their names, their culture, their homes, their relatives, their family, traditions, and religion, which was excessively big to them. At the same time, not the slaves but the thieves who stole them went to church. They prayed for good weather for growing food. They prayed for a safe journey across the Atlantic. Their prayers were for their profit. You put any name to it, and they lost it when they were captured. I've said it once, and I'll probably repeat it, what was their crime? In my opinion, none whatsoever. Just unfortunate to be caught up by some ruthless men, who with the opportunity of profit at the end, stole from them.

You may well ask if you can trace your family back for any length of time. I cannot, a few years ago, I picked up the telephone directory in Barbados—yes, there is only one. This contains all the names of residents who subscribe to landlines. In it, you could well be reading a directory full of subscribers the size of Hampshire in England, for the names therein are the same as they are in the south of England.

My name is *Hunte*, ending with an "e." My thinking is that it could have come down via the last man who would have been the "owner" of my great-grandmother. This is slavery I am referring to and the aftermath of it.

A law banning the transporting of slaves was passed in London in 1843. However, it was not illegal to own slaves, so breeding was introduced by the owners, and their offspring were sold. Others lived as animals, down on the beach in makeshift shacks, covered with leaves cut from the coconut trees, the leaves pointing down so that the rainwater ran off and towards the ground. Life on the plantation from what I can see, from my findings, is that there were no houses provided for the slaves.

Over in America, the slaves were marched to work and marched out at the end of the day's work; they were mustered up and walked back to their pens along with the animals. Something terribly similar took place in Europe where the animals slept downstairs. The humans were upstairs. That way, more heat was produced in the building. The humans were on hand to keep the animals safe should there be any attempted raids on the livestock.

The end of slavery came into force in Barbados in 1834; it was one year later that the Royal Police Force was formed to police ex-slave owners. So for that first year after the end of slavery, there would have been no law at all. It's not that hard to see why some form of reprisals took place. The courts were managed along the same lines as they were in England. I am thinking in those days, any smart, clever young man with a little knowledge of the law, could pinch a blonde wig and kit himself out as a barrister.

What's in a Name?

The proportion of land in the island of Barbados is 166 square miles. Its fertile land made the island a goldmine for the British. This is partly because the topsoil in some places is just two feet deep; it has a "honeycomb type" structure, which can hold water long after the rain has fallen.

So now, we're not only the slaves imprisoned by the sea but also the former slave owners, with nowhere to hide. The overseers would have thought their days were numbered. The rich and the poor lived in remarkable proximity. It would have been like living in a goldfish bowl. A long history of distrust and grievances provided the opportunity for some payback.

The men and women who were in charge of the overseers, to exercise his power, carried out beating because he could do so. A few slavers would have, could have, made plans, in doubt carried some of them out. The slavers owners could not have seen the end was in sight, for the supreme power was shifting. In England, the House of Commons day after day was in an uproar. Some of the members were also slave owners.

The slaves and the ex-owners were in a muddle at a time of uncertainty. Without any law or lawmakers or law enforcers, it would have been like hell on earth, for the men and women, even though now free of bondage. It was an uncertain time for all, rich and poor alike. Slave and slave master had equal billing. Both now had the same status, that of being "free" in this lawless land.

As a young man, I felt trapped on the island, like fish in a goldfish in a bowl. I was swimming around as though in prison. Yes, I saw some of the ill treatment of some, even as late as the 1940s. My aunt Doots saw the hopelessness in me; I think she saw me like a goldfish out of the bold. She offered me a way out, a passage to England. I jumped at it and promised to repay her and that I did. I arrived at

Southampton on September 2, 1960. I worked on the buses, as I had worked for a bus company in Barbados.

I did that for a couple of months. Then I joined the army on November 29, 1960. It was what I wanted to do. As far as I was concerned, a soldier is a man or woman who can stand tall. I volunteered to join the army when other men were running away from it. It is possible they knew something I did not know. Probably from their fathers or experience of what was going on in the press at the time. I received none of that, so fear did not enter any of my thinking. I wanted to, and I did, join at my own free will.

My six years in the army was like a university to me. All the things that I've learned came into play sometime later in life. Like when I was homeless, it was my army skills that kept me alive. I slept on every major station in London. Understanding some of that time, I was working, I would get into Paddington to unlock my locker to get my shaving kit out, down into the gents' for a quick shave, and I was back up into the locker, and off again, not knowing where I'd be sleeping when night fell.

By looking after others, one stands in the way of bombs and bullets and is willing to give his life so that others can carry on with their way of life.

CHAPTER 9

ALONE WITHOUT LAWS

Once more I have concluded that power is like beauty and age—it's on loan. We are beautiful when we're young, and as we get older, it wears off—the debt is paid. To me, it's the same thing with power, only holding it for a given time. People with power live in big houses; this shows their status, wealth, and sometimes stupidity. Their wealth is on display. Take that away, and they are just like you and me—one heartbeat away from death, the same as you or I.

I draw my conclusions from the German soldiers who tried to hide at the end of the Second World War. Allied forces started to close in on them; they all ran and hid like rats when they saw the power ebbing away from them. When your ability leaves you, and those around you tend to see the consequences before you can, they hide it from you. There were two others, and one was Gadhafi, a powerful man with a big rifle, who ended up buried in a dugout when soldiers found him. Adolf Hitler is another; he blamed the people of Germany, who he accused of letting him down. He had no idea of what he had started, and then he could not continue. He wasn't brave enough to say, "I have led you and I lost." History is full of such men who got led away by the alexia of power.

As at the end of slavery, master and once slave would have had equal rights. One day, you were a slave; the next day, you were free to roam the tiny island. You wouldn't have had any friends, and everything would be new to you as you congregated toward Bridgetown or Speightstown. They were the two most significant towns on the island at the time, depending on which part of the island you were on when freedom came. Now let's look at the facts: there would have been no transport apart from maybe a horse and a cart to get from one place to another. Some of these places may have been familiar during their lives on the island, but now they had to survive on their own, use their wits, with no job and no income. Some workers may have been asked to stay on by the farmers or landowners. This could have been the first time some workers were paid for their labor.

One day a slave, the next a free man or woman. Most of them had worked doing manual labor all their lives, and only the fittest survived. Their owners and managers would have been physically smaller compared with the six-foot Africans. The average Englishman in the seventeenth century was about five foot three. So they would have ruled with fear and violence, with a rifle, a shotgun, and a bullwhip in hand. Obviously, we know the threats made to misbehaving slaves; some suffered by being boiled in sugar and other inhumane crimes.

The Romans did leave England and run most of the county for many years. It would have become a lawless society, so much so the men would be with horns on their head. They came and started to run amok, imposing their state of law. The next time, in my opinion, was 1945, Germany and in Japan, after the bomb landed in Hiroshima and Nagasaki. This would also have happened in a few lawless states after the leader is deposed, executed, or imprisoned. We find in our research that a troublesome time always follows, and it can take years before laws are established. I mean that there will be winners and losers; some that had top jobs before, could now become beggars. I think this occurred when students started humiliating teachers and lecturers. I think you will know of others in history like this, if not they can be researched.

Revolution also brings this to the victor—the spoils.

The invaders of another person's land always must leave and go home. It doesn't matter how long they stay; eventually, they will have to leave. Leaders never seem to see the end coming. If you don't like the leader and they push you around too much, always keep it in the back of your mind that they will have to go, sooner or later. From what I can see, from previous events in the country that they invaded, they try to impose their laws and customs on the people whom they invaded.

With the law of England six thousand miles away across the Atlantic, Barbados was a lawless place for a time. My grandmother and others had to endure a lawless society. The island would have been tough to live on at that time. As I said earlier, there was a gap between the end of slavery and the police force being formed. My grandmother was a charming, lovely-looking woman with smooth skin. She had nothing to be happy about, yet she maintained her dignity as head of the house. Now I can see why she was that way; she had been beaten into submission and worn down by it all. Her three daughters were the joy of her life. It has taken me all these years to realize the woman she was and what she meant to me, and I to her. As her first grandson, a joy for the woman looking back to the village, Carrington Village, Bridgetown, Barbados—the place of my birth.

A glass of rum, as the sun went down at each day's end. Rum is known worldwide as coming from the West Indies. But I'll give it to the Scotsmen who were ordered to evict the land after the mammoth uprising from May to July 1685. About seven hundred men and women were transported to the West Indies. Those who had worked in the making of whiskey now had the juice of the sugarcane! They used the sugarcane juice and distilled it down to make rum, using their know-how of whiskey-making as it was done in Scotland.

Rum was made in the same way, adding a bit of caramel and some spices. Alcohol from rotting fruit has been and is still man's favorite drink. It can be made from almost any fruit of a living plant. It can and has been used as an antiseptic wash for cuts or burns and to protect against infections. Rum was produced in Brazil and Cuba, but Barbados was the first country to make a profit from the production of rum. In 1740, rum was introduced to the Royal Navy. I traveled on a naval ship, took my place, and was issued rum and water known to the troop as half and half. I arrived at the conclusion that Lord Nelson ordered the rum for the Navy from Barbados, not him personally but his quartermaster because his ships were clean in Bridgetown, Barbados. The method of making sugar was very successfully tried and tested both in Brazil and Cuba. In fact, plantations owners would have imported cane from India, having seen that potential, for sugar in Europe.

The mongoose was introduced to Barbados in the 1870s. Snacks had hitched a ride hidden among the cane and became pets, the workers who work in the field planting and later harvesting the cane. A snake bite could lead to death as there was no anti-venom for snake bites in Barbados.

The British then took it to Barbados. The climate was pleasant, and it thrived in the weather. With sunshine and rainfall throughout the year, it multiplied year by year. Barbados was one of the most significant sugar supplier to British economy, which lasted well into the sixties white sugar king.

Grandmother used to take her rum straight—one glut and it was gone. She would hold the small glass in her right hand, thumb, and forefinger and raise it to her mouth. When the glass touched her lips, back would go her head. When her head returned, the glass was empty—a shot of rum straight, no chaser, from her sherry glass. The harshness of the drink would register on her face, as I watched her, and recorded it in my subconscious. Now I am older. I understand the pain and hardship she lived with.

Taking a nip of rum from a small glass that was probably brought to the island by the English, Irish, or Scottish families as they sailed in, to start a life in the sun was her way of reducing the pain of her lot. It would have been used for celebrating—for example, wetting the baby's head. We had an excellent drink of rum for all occasions—a birth, or a death, to commemorate a life.

Oliver Cromwell had a few thousand people transported off the shores of England in the 1600s. He was tired of killing, and the smell of death must have gotten to him. A few hundred Irishmen were sent to Barbados as a punishment to become white slaves. Some were sold to work in the fields alongside black slaves. There are still descendants living on the island today.

Emancipation came to the men and women in Barbados in 1834. I was born one hundred and seven years after liberation. I could well have been a slave had I been born earlier. Going back a bit, I can see that my grandmother would have been in the mix of things. Today, we call it ethnic cleansing, but then it was getting rid of the unwanted. When the "laird" said, "Do as I say," you did it or did as you saw fit. Seeing fit to do for some was booking passage to the USA. This was the way some people managed to get real "freedom."

CHAPTER 10

THE CHATTEL HOUSES

These houses, like the one that I lived in as a child, were a bit like a flat pack. They can be dismantled and taken to another plot of land, put back together by about six to ten men in one day. The sides are V-shaped and will accommodate the roof, which is covered in wooden shingles. These sloping sides allow the water to drain away. The V-shaped shingles are laid overlapping, just as slate tiles on a roof would be. The thick part of the shingle was about a quarter of an inch and nailed to slats with flat nonrust nails. This type of house could be very quickly blown away when those yearly hurricanes came, and they came year after year. The design was weak, and many of the wooden houses were blown away. They were never designed and built to be storm-proof, just some shelter for the workers.

Things moved along the 1940s, and war seemed to have taken up most of the talk and energy at the time. Food was hard to come by, just homegrown sweet potato, yams, and fruits.

The German U-boats cruised up and down the Atlantic, sinking cargo ships and playing havoc with the shipping that helped to keep the British war program going. America and Canada ships now started to sail in larger numbers across the Atlantic, making less of a target for the Garman U-boats.

Food caned and tried to feed the people, including oil and rubber of the UK. Fortune began to favor allied forces. They gained the upper hand of the Germans. This was the turning point in Britain favor.

I was with my mother in Bridgetown, Barbados, where this upside-down boat was tied up. I now know it one of the German U-Boat 514 series. I was four years old at the time. At the tender years, I could not understand why only a part was showing. Men were standing, moving on it, and it was not sinking. I was in the opposite of the careenage with my mother. This would have been, to the best of my knowledge, 1945. I can still see it clearly; we would have been closes to Lord Nelson Coolum.

The massive slow-moving laden convoys en route to the docks in Britain passed us on their way from the USA and Canada, crossing the Atlantic. We had to cope by using every bit of land on our island for growing food.

There was a plant that grew by the roadside that we used to make tea from it. I don't think I ever knew the name of it. Supplies of tea and other food stuffs just dried up, as they would all have come from Britain. Some of the boxes of tea were part payment for sugar and cotton that was grown on the island. Don't think for a minute that it was free, it was hard-earned in cane and cotton. Over two hundred years of slave labor and all the riches were shipped off to Britain.

I once helped my mother pick cotton, not in the fields but in a building of steel. It was named the steel shade. The women had to clean it of all the impurities. The leaves, buds, and twigs had to be removed. Wet hands were not allowed. Some women used to wet their hands as they cleaned the cotton. I don't know if the cotton was grown in Barbados or if it was brought in to be picked and washed. It was a very dull job, sitting picking the bits of dried leaves and bits of twigs. Then put in crocus bags to be weighed, and the woman would be given a ticket from the cashier as a record of how much was earned. Today, crocus bags are used for an assortment of things, even plant pots. In the seventeenth century, it was used for slave clothing.

CHAPTER 11

THE AFTER YEARS

As the years rolled by one after another, the light began to show in my education, how lacking it was and how little I had learned. The school I attended was St. Giles Boys' School; it was a school for the poor of the island. The money for the schools to be built came from sugar, so when I mentioned my grandmother working in the cane fields, I think you can join the two together and end up with your answer.

I don't know if it was taught or even referred to in school, to ten-year-olds about the war. Yet some would have lived through it, losing their homes and family members. I did get some private teaching for a while from an ex-teacher earning some extra money. She used her house to give lessons to a few kids, helping to get them ready for school. My mother took me there to get prepared for the big school. On reflection, it was a waste of money. For when it came to attending St. Giles Boys' School, I cried like a baby when she walked away and left me in the schoolyard. It was a terrifying experience—one I don't think I ever got over. There was no showing me around first or welcoming. It was just walking right in without preparation—it haunted me. Everything looked so significant to me; the school ground was big and spacious, Today, it does not seem so big when I have returned to look at it. I've wondered why I was so afraid, but I was only five years old then.

By 1951, I was a schoolboy of ten years old. Life was hard as I mentioned before and still was hard. I am saying it once more as it hurts me to remember. I cannot stop the pain of that time. There were many displaced men, women, and children in Europe. Men had returned but not all of them. Some paid with their lives. Those who made it, the few that came back, were shipped off to Cuba instead of their home islands and were labelled as troublemakers. How come when a man or woman starts to fight for his or her rights, they became troublemakers? These would have experienced some cold winters when dressed in their tropical kit. The long cold winters followed at the end of the bombing. Is thought, to have been caused by what was in the bombs from both sides of the conflict.

No one currently was talking about the world's weather, satellite, and global communication was not yet in use. These words were still to be added to our language sometime after the war. The scenes men who designed and built the doodlebugs, that fell on London, and other parts of the UK, they were now working on getting a man onto the moon! By rights, all these men were war criminals. They should have been tried for war crimes. A paper clip was attached to some of the documents. These men were processed as being given specific jobs, so they walked free. They had an offer to work, from the men they had been shooting and trying to kill.

CHAPTER 12

HIGH WINDS BLOW OVER BARBADOS

In 1955, a hurricane by the name of Janet ripped through the Caribbean, blowing and spinning its way past the island, reaching over one hundred miles an hour as it passed over. It flattened everything in its path. Barbados caught the tail end of its power as it passed by. Men, women, and children were all running to the shelter. Ours was the school, St. Giles Boys' School on Ivy Road. The rain was coming down fast and furious; the dark clouds hung menacingly over Ivy Village where I was lived at the time. The wind was blowing wild and violently; paper and trash from the cane fields spewed everywhere. Lightning flashed through the dark clouds; I was very reluctant to go to the shelter. I just strolled along, as if walking in the park on a Sunday afternoon. I was fourteen years old, and at that age, I thought I was indestructible!

As I walked from my home, I saw sheets of corrugated roofing ripped from the houses by the strong winds. They were carried in the wind like sheets of paper. It was dark as night, and yet, it was still daytime, with fast-rolling clouds violently crossing the sky. I had time to look up, for I was not running. I don't think I knew fear or the danger I was in at that time.

Some six feet of galvanized corrugated metal sheets were flying about, like sheets of paper. I was walking toward St. Giles Boys' School, which was our shelter, my school. People run and called out to others; women carried small children on their hips. Small children clutched the hands of parents and older siblings, running as fast as their legs would take them. The wind was strong. One must grip tightly, carrying along with necessities that would be needed. Old men and women made their way as best they could to the shelter. I kept my eyes on the flying bits of wood. I was willing the corrugated sheets to stay out of the way if they seemed to be coming at me. I still took my time, watching as the tall palm and coconut trees bent in the wind. Some were even uprooted and crashed into houses, blocking the road as they fell. The distance from my home to the shelter was less than half a mile.

The next day, the storm had died down. We all tried to inspect the damage. Our house was still standing. Others were not so fortunate. Some livestock was not walking and looking for food; some black-bellied sheep were found high in the trees over net feet high. They were carried there by water from the one river on the island. Calm had returned to the island. Some of the sheep made the noise they would make when hungry or lost. It's possible to research the details of Hurricane Janet in 1955 on the internet and find out the route it took as it spun its way up and down the Caribbean Sea. There are photos there, just one of the many things that the internet has brought to us.

The types of houses in the island can be picked up like a doll's house, blown about and smashed to smithereens, resulting in a pile of kindling. It's all part of the Atlantic hurricane season, which blows up every year. However, the flat-packed houses were ill-designed for these strong winds, so the hurricane season was a trial for everyone. That ill-wind that blew was not prejudiced. Everyone ended up taking shelter in the school. We slept on chairs and on the floor. I could write about it until the cows come home. I can only give you my personal experience—just how devastating it was for me and why I ran away. This was not a joint pack I made with another; it was only my force by the pain I often receive with no one I could call upon. On reflection, it was child abuse, and then when the wind died down, the calm arrived over everything. I made it against the odds.

Could I have known that from the start? I don't think so. He who runs with the pack commands respect?

CHAPTER 13

THE MEMORIES OF GROWING UP

The war had wrapped itself right around the world. The First World War was terrible as we know, then came the Second World War, and that was even worse. People who had no right to vote, for people who were colonized by the nations who were fighting, suffered more than any other in my opinion. If you think about the role, that rubber played in the Second World War. So long as you have vehicles working on the roads, you will need rubber. Wherever the suppliers of rubber were, they had no rights to vote whether there would be war or not.

The oil producers in Africa, again living under the British, had no rights in voting. They also grew the food that was shipped to the UK. Docks such as Liverpool, Bristol, and London were heavily engaged in unloading the food that came across the Atlantic from India, not forgetting Canada, Australia, and New Zealand—they all supplied food. Those countries just mentioned sent women to fight and nurse the injured back to health.

Men came from the Caribbean to join the RAF. Some had never flown in a plane, but they helped to maintain them. Men and women in the Caribbean collected money for the war contribution. Women living in the Caribbean who had never experienced cold fingers were knitting gloves for their men. That alone speaks volumes for all walks of women from the Caribbean. They contributed by knitting for those with frozen fingers, so severe that they could not grip or hold anything.

That alone makes me wonder, how can you conclude what it is going to feel like in a cold climate when you come from the West Indies? The women would put their fingers into the gloves they had knitted. It was beyond their comprehension how cold it could be, yet they delivered, by knitting gloves for the men.

Growing up, the rail line was my playground. There were no trains, and we kids living in Barbados played under the rail tracks or what was left of them. I say that because the train tracks were taken and shipped back to England. The iron was needed so the war minster put out a call. The railway lines that were laid in Barbados were not laid for passengers. It was to carry the sugar to the docks to be loaded on ships set for England. I was there some years ago and went to the library to see where the trains ran. There was only one train, and it ran from Bathsheba to Bridgetown. As I said, I had not seen them myself. Being born in 1941, they were already gone, but some tracks were still there.

CHAPTER 14

CLEAR BLUE SEAWATER

In Barbados, walking along the clear beach water, as fresh as the day, leaving my footprints with every step that I take, only to be washed away with the next breaking wave—that is beach life.

This was my playground as I was growing up on the island, the water always fresh and bright in the early-morning sun. Small fish with blur backs, no bigger than my index finger, can be seen feeding in the sand of the water's edge. The small sandpiper also feeds there, running up and down as the waves come in and out. Out of curiosity, I tried to find out the species of sandpiper there is on Barbados on the internet. I type in "sandpiper"; it gives me a list of hotels. That alone tells me how widespread the bird sandpiper is in Barbados. They are where the land is kissed by the sea. It's a joy to watch, as the waves come, one after another, washing away my footprints. I walk in the warm on top and cool clear above water warmed by the sun my barefoot along the beach. Early in the morning, after a raging storm the night before, the sea gives off a fresh, clean scent and sea spray that is like a mist. I have only ever experienced this on a few other beaches in my travels. One such was in Mombasa, the water kissing the sand the same as in Barbados. It is as if the sea purges itself, as the storm inevitably comes every year.

The native flowers are ones that must have "hooked" a ride on the floating driftwood over thousands of years. They would be in the Atlantic, looking for a place to anchor. Much the same as plastic does today, sadly. The hibiscus is the national flower of Barbados. It was when I was a boy. It heads up from Mexico, bobbing along with the tide, on its way up from Florida Keys for years and years. Floating on the water as the wind to its destination. Like the coconut, it can get to the Isle of Arran in Scotland and take root and feed on freshwater.

Today, there is a floating mass of cork, wood, plastic bottles, toothbrushes and toilet seats, and toys, all made from various materials. Some are man-made while the rest from natural plant waste, carried along by the tide, looking to dock. In a few hundred years, there might be an island with plants and birds in the Pacific made of plastic and plants. I'll say that the sea can take it, as it harmlessly bobs up and down with the tide. The earth, like our bodies, has an underwritten contract to look after itself; however, with too many poisons, it will fall victim to damage.

I have a written record of the date that I lost my father. It was February 27, 1984, the day of his passing. Then I had to "get brave" in my thinking and do what I hadn't before, to be responsible. It was not so much the loss of him, as he was not much of a father to me. I cannot tell you one thing we did together, not one single trick did I learn from him. When I met him, I was a young man of nineteen years. I met him at Waterloo station. That was after he had sailed the broad Atlantic on an old Spanish ship. He lived with his wife in Chapel Market, Islington, North London. This was my first address in the city.

The smell of a man was what was missing, from my growing years. Also, no skills had I learned from him, not how to tie my shoelaces or other skills I would need. As I grew older and reflected on this, I think it's terrible. We learn by watching others. We emulate them and their movements, their mannerisms. Other things you learn from your mother's apron strings. You learn how to cook, discover the power of fire and force and water and wind. When there's no one to learn from, you're on your own. I was on my own. This is the first time I have to admit this, but I was unwanted as a child. I was not dumped in the trash bin. I was just left alone, a bit like a sea turtle who finds its way to either sink or swim.

The smell is one of our strongest senses we grew up with. It remembers job wood paint or aftershave, to be able to watch him comb his beard or shave and smell the aftershave his face. I have nothing to remember. I was shaving one morning, and my daughter came into the bathroom to fetch something. She saw me putting foam on my face, and she wanted some on her face. It's about having someone to learn from. Whether you use those skills that you learned from watching or not, that does not matter. You have them, you know of them, you can use them if it applies or not if it doesn't.

When I received my orders to report to a camp, it came by post. The first thing I did was to go out and buy a shaving set, razor, and shaving stick. I felt sure that this would make me a man.

The war had left the world short of men, young and old. London had been thumped by the devastation of the German bombs, the damage still visible and very much evident when I arrived in the 1960s. It is far easier to destroy than to build; it falls faster than it rises. That is obvious even for me to see, the destruction of the bombing twenty-six years later.

The city was short of young men and women. The empire was already lost; it's purpose was domination over millions of people.

When they asked for help from men and women who had lived in appalling conditions, they were now being asked to come and fight. What's more, they came and fought to prove that equal rights were needed between men and women. The changes would happen, but it seems to me, that those in power were so firmly rooted in their power that they thought they could prevent alteration, but change will happen and has!

When a man or woman goes to war, he or she is changed by it, whether it's the smell of burning. Be it just fire feeding on what it ignites, be it be wood paint or bodies. Or knows more than in any other circumstances. It shapes the young life that is flowering after the two world wars, men that went off to fight and had to leave some of their friends on the battlefields.

I was told by my commanding officer, not to mention to men replacing what had happened to me and a few others within the hills of the Radfan. When we were on our way back to the camp in Bahrain, we were given a lecture at Komatsu airport. We were not to say in any way what we had experienced in the hills. Some of my kit was shot to pieces. It was never replaced. I had to buy new equipment, regions I should have a claim when I was there.

I think the same thing could have been issued to the men and women at the end of the war, both wars.

That six years I spent in the army was like my time at university. I could not have gained that experience anyplace else. It was a bit of everything I mentioned, including racial prejudice outside the building outside the church in Reims in France. How I had to run for my life in the camp in the boxing ring the young men were throwing beach blocks at me. I just had to duck and dive as they come hurtling across the apron of the boxing ring.

CHAPTER 15

THE LONG ROAD

L iving is like traveling a road, a new turning in the road every day. You make a turn on the hope that it is the best one to make. It doesn't always turn out the right way, and sometimes you must make corrections to get back on the track intended.

I'm speaking of the road from boyhood to manhood. You only pass it once, how and where you end up can and will depend on a lot of things and a lot of people. To have a man so that you could emulate him could be extremely helpful. Without that someone, I was lost in a sea of towering waves—just myself and a sea of sharks of people. Givers and takers, you must make a choice. That choice can result in sink or swim, each day as it unfolds.

With more bumps on the road to adulthood and the hardships they can cause as they inevitably do, those bumps are hard on the back. Every walkway has its hazards. The knocks and kicks I encountered were more than I had planned for. A duck will likely find a pond, where it fits with other ducks. For myself, with just a dream to go on, I needed a bit more. As I started on my goal, I stood on the sandy shores of Barbados, gazing out into the Atlantic Ocean, dreaming, with no one to guide me.

I took a few chances that came my way. Some were right for me; others, I had to pay the price. Yes, the road I took was long, hard, and rough, and I needed some support along the way. I could have gone on making mistakes indefinitely, but I received some help from the most unexpected quarters. Fortunately, I had a helping hand now and then.

Like the sergeant who asked me to come in one Saturday morning and finish my exam papers although all the test papers had been handed in on Friday evening. He had a quick read through and saw that I was not up to standard. He had a word in my ear and put me right. Life was extremely hard for me as it was for lots of others, I'm sure. I just had to find my own way forward, making my own rules as to what to do and how to do it. If you had someone to guide you, you probably would not know what it was like for someone like me. I hope you understand when I use the word *guide*, it's more of a pathway or someone showing you the way. It was and is awfully hard. Had I known just how long and hard it was going to be, I might have opted out and stayed as the beachcomber that I was as a boy. With all the hills I had to climb on my way, obstacle after obstacle, popping up to try to block me. At times, I had to seek another route, with no one to turn to or to ask for advice. I just had to move with the flow, duck, and dive, learn on the job whatever the situation happened to be at the time, and there were quite a few like that.

In the real sense of the word, I am a pathfinder. To find a way forward, I would always see and feel how the wind was blowing. With no map to guide me, I was on my own, in every sense of the word. I have always had a sort of fascination with strangers that I meet for the first time. When they hear how I speak English and where I come from, my reply astonishes most of them. Some have looked at me in wonder, as to how I made it thus far. It's no wonder to me. I just did what I had to do. I used what I was given, some of my intentions, and some hard work, no more and no less. Well, perhaps with a sprinkle of magic. When the magic comes, you will know it, for it comes from unexpected places at unexpected moments. You just must be ready. When you're ready, you just must go with the flow and believe in yourself and the magic.

CHAPTER 16

A SORT OF WORD BLINDNESS

I am dyslexic. I discovered late about dyslexia, well, after I had left school and had travelled halfway across the world to England. Once there, I joined the army, and still, it was not discovered. It was all hands on deck; the army was short of young men. National service had ended, and so regular soldiers were offered a trade and better pay. I took the test and passed; I did not get the deal I wanted as it required more education than I had at the time.

I was at school and was put down as being stupid. Dyslexia was not on the school lookout list, nor was it on the army's list, what's more. It was thirty-five years after the war when I found out what my problem was. I was in my late thirties by the time it was discovered. Words can play tricks on my eyes; I think the letters keep moving place. I read, and they seem to jump about on the pages. My spelling is a bit hard to comprehend, the vernacular of the spoken language. The characteristics can vary from person to person. One day I can spell a word and then the next day I cannot. I keep plodding at reading, I am better with visual things because I need to analyze the words, almost every word, as to how the writer meant it to be read.

When I was at school, the teachers probably did not know what it was. At school, I was treated as a dunce. I could not read or take dictation. I tended to pick up on the ends of words. I didn't know my eight times table; it is one that still eludes me today. However, I do know my ten times table.

Leaving school at the tender age of thirteen, I could not read or write. Something was wrong, but no one told me. I was just treated as dumb. Being treated that way, I began to think, that was my lot in life, for the rest of my life. So leaving school was the beginning of my learning of the world and what goes on in it. I started to learn from the fishermen, going out with them and returning in the afternoon. The men worked unloading the schooners with produce from some of the other islands. Mostly fresh fruit, mangoes, plantains, yams, and sweet potatoes. Young black fit-looking boys, with trim bodies, biceps were bulging the skin, displaying their physique. As they swam before they dived for coins, which were tossed in the water by wealthy tourists, as they waited to dock on land from the launch bringing them ashore. The world and its faraway areas became my source of curiosity; people and their faces had become my classroom. Being dyslexic had given me a little something to work with, and that must have helped. It could have made me a bit fearless, as my reply to most challenges was why? Why not?

To think I was once on my deathbed! Death was about to walk in on me, with just hours to live, the poison was racing through my body and killing me. Someone from the hospital must have called, or got a message to my mother. We had no telephone at home. I just don't know, but there she was, my mother. I say called, we are armed with the mobile phone today, but back in the fifties, it was only in comic books. Such things, the words *mobile* and *phone* were not in use as they are today. So they called my mother to see me, her first son and say goodbye. Unknown to me, a guardian angel was hovering and looking after me; death made a wrong call to me, too early a call. Dying, as you can tell from me still kicking, went away, as I am still here today. It cannot be written off, just the timing of it. I remained in good health, to the high standard of fitness that was required and demanded to complete "P Coy" in the winter of 1961. It's a course. It is said to be one of the hardest courses designed by man for man, both mentally and physically.

The Brecon Beacons mountain ranges are in South Wales. They will remember me as I do them. The January weather can drop to twenty-one degrees Fahrenheit. The icicles seemed to grow on the bracken, as I passed them. They were five to six inches long (I know of no women who have taken the course). You can see what the course involves by looking it up on the internet. There's a good description there. It has been polished up since I passed and it is quite different today from what I can see. If I had known how hard it was before going, I might have said, it's not for me, but I am thrilled I did it.

If you have a smartphone, all right let's face it, nearly every school kid has them today. I travel on the train a lot, and something like ten out of ten people has their phones on them. So as I was saying, you can easily find out more about dyslexia. You will also find out the famous who are dyslexic.

CHAPTER 17

I BELIEVE IN THEM

Having a dream is to believe in one that keeps returning, that is a way forward. It's your subconscious at work. You can name your vision, and you can put yourself in the mix. If you have dreams, you may see those dreams come to fruition.

As a person, I think you must believe them. I see it as part of life. We dream, so do cats and dogs, maybe lions also, and many other living creatures. To imagine that I might see my dreams happen. It's the subconscious and works best at night when we are asleep.

Most of my friends are men, but when I need help, it's a woman I turn to. Yes, I had men friends that I would turn to when I needed help. I slept on quite a few settees in my time when I was homeless. I was homeless for a few months. It was a painful time for me, for some of that time I was working. I got caught up in the system. Sleeping rough is no fun. My face used to be swollen in the mornings from the cold winds blowing through the station. Waterloo, Paddington, Victoria, and Liverpool Street—I once knew all the hiding places.

At Paddington, I kept my shaving kit in a locker. In the morning, I would get it out and go and shave in the washroom, then return the equipment to the steel locker. With my weekly pay, I bought new clothes. It was horrible living that way. Thankfully, it did not last long.

We can all talk of miracles, rant about them. Either you believe in them or you don't. I happened to be down and out; some lousy management meant that I was about to lose my home. I owed thousands of pounds in mortgage arrears. A letter dropped on the mat, and like so many men, I just left it and hoped it would go away. In the end, I had to move and move fast. There was a notice given, then the final date for payment was almost upon me, even down to the last few hours. Then I called a friend and told her. "I can let you have the money," she told me. There were only twenty hours until I would have to hand in the keys. I ran to the office where I made my monthly payments, but when I got there, it was closed. The women in the building society were exceptionally good at understanding my situation. When I explained my predicament, they took my payment.

I was later told that a house was bought with me in mind, should I ever become homeless, by a perfect female friend.

I have lived in a home with four women, wife and four daughters. There were moods and a lot of knickers, but that is life with no other men about. Growing up, I was just too young to know about these things. It's only later in my life, when looking back, that I understand. You have to learn some of the meaning to the slang do what the cockneys say, duck and dive, to fit in, or as they say, go with the flow.

Bypassing the "P. Coy" course, I was initiated into the maroon beret. This was proof if ever I needed it. All I had was my dream and a will to live it. Did I do it? Yes, I did. Not once but twice. On a night march across Brecon, I twisted my felt ankle. When we got to a village, we took a rest. I took off my boots from the left foot. That was it. Like a balloon, it has swollen twice its regular size. I could not get my wet boot back on my foot. I made the mistake of taking it off when I tried the fit the boot on, the swelling had enlarged.

It felt like the end of the road for me so I could go any farther. My world started to fall apart. The dream began to fade, the winds showed me no favors could do help. This was the Brecon beaches. It has a feast reputation, probably as much as the Eiger.

The meds were called, and they got me about one, and later, I had to sit in the cold and wait. I received some strange look from passing farmers.

I do believe in quite a lot, to think that a man could be seen walking on water or that he could turn water into wine. That may take some believing unless I tasted it. Today, we have got a lot smarter, and we expect proof before believing.

CHAPTER 18

SKIN COLOR AS THE STATUS

Looking at a photo of my grandfather, you will see that he has some European blood in his genes.

Skin color matters. A black man or woman could be first in line for a job interview. The job would be taken, even though you were first in the front. This was the kind of preconceived judgment that was used in the 1960s, probably well before then, but that's when I experienced it. Prejudice starts in the home, the playground, and the workplace.

Skin matters quite a lot, after all, the empire was fed from the labor of slaves. Most of the privileged people in England at the time were living a carefree life. The ships arrived, the food was downloaded into the shops, and no questions were asked about where it came from. Coconuts were mostly seen in fairgrounds; it was a novelty to shoot a coconut. They would have known that it came from a tropical island, the dried coconut would be used in sweets. Indeed, no one asked where the sugar came from or how high it grew before being harvested. They did not know, and they did not care. They just took it for granted.

It was the same with cotton, made into cloth and sold as cotton fabric. The small island of Barbados produced both cotton and sugarcane. I don't think it was part of the lesson plan at school, as to where the sugar came from. That would come later, around 1974, when there was a sugar strike. In Britain, sugar was in high demand, more so than now, for it has been accused of causing ill health, mainly in young people.

CHAPTER 19

HEALTHY GENES HAVE BEEN GIVEN

I carry the genes of the African slave men and women who were taken from their homes and shipped across the Atlantic into slavery. Through natural selection, Mother Nature had a hand in preserving the gene. The genes were always there; it was finding out about DNA that played catch-up. Today, they can be traced right back to who we are and where we came from, unlike our names that got lost in ownership. We find another man thinks of the illusion that he can own somebody by giving them a name. That is a false belonging, but to survive, I'm sure some of us had to play along.

In my seventy-nine years, I have been hospitalized once, which I recorded earlier. I am living proof of my standing. It could have been some sort of horse injection they gave me, I have no idea. Whatever it was, it worked for me. Do we need to be told what's in it when we're vaccinated? Or injected at the dentist or in the hospital? We are never told what is in it. If we were sat down and explained in layman's language, could we begin to understand the complexity of the mixed? I don't think so.

This must be taken very seriously, for doctors have used drugs on black men in the southern states of the USA for testing on. They tested those on sick men without them knowing it. I know a similar sort of experiment was used in Germany in the 1940s. A few madmen and women wanted to be able to say that they had created a super healthy person. I am glad that it's more likely that there would be a super moving, working robot. That is a more feasible way out.

I have experienced just another day other in hospital since then, after testing for a cancer operation. I often wonder if something in that injection, over sixty years ago, has kept me in good health.

The body is one massive organ. Like anything that works, it needs to be maintained. I now take care of my intake of food and drink. As a young man in the army, no one warned us about our health. It is well known that the armed forces drink and can overdo it at times. I did it quite often in my youth. We used to meet up in the pub and drink about five or six pints a night and think nothing of it. The consequences of such action could and did catch up on us in later life. Maybe they didn't expect us to live for exceptionally long, for there is nothing like an old soldier.

Apparently, when a man sees death, it has been said that it gives him something to live for. Seeing a close friend get shot or blown up by a bomb or a wire or a booby trap, you have to keep moving, because there could be a second one with your name on it. It's tough to leave a roommate, but at times, survival kicks in, and you must move on. Something kicks in. I think it's adrenaline. It gives you the drive and will to go on. Soldiering is a team job. You live and work together as one. You always rely on the man next to you, in camp and on the battlefield. Yet there comes a time when you may have to run and leave your best mate if he gets shot. We become more robust as a team, to win as one, not to go down in one heap. The training is so hard that when the fighting started, every man would play their part.

If the training is adequately worked out, you would continually be doing the same thing, day in and day out. Then when the fighting starts, every man knows where he is and where he should be, also the man next to him. How come shy young men as I was then found the courage to jump out of an airplane at night? It's all to do with the bean trained to do so—it's synthetic training. This, I will add, is long before a flight simulator that is used today, was invented.

This is the art of teamwork, before jumping out of an airplane. You check the man in front of you, last in line, turn and has his equipment, by the one but last, to make sure everything is in order, for when the green light comes on, or a tap on your shoulder, that's an order, and it's your turn to go. You would be tapped on the shoulder and, in some cases, were pushed out into the slipstream.

Jumping in the summer evening over the plane, you can see the DZ. A night jump not much to see other than the lights far away. Your training comes in to play. The drill is not to reach for the grown and let it come up to meet you.

When you get that call to stand up and the hand actions going up means you stand up. The next order would be hooked up, so you hook your strapline, your hook, your trap get a strong point in the airplane that runs along the fuselage. There's a strange March you do that is you move the back foot first. There would be an under-jump sergeant holding the first one at the door the green line would come on there is that tap on your shoulder you jumped and the next one, on the next one, on the next one. As you lay there the slipstream, you can hear the nylon thread popping. This is the canopy, opening. You lie there with your hands across the chest slipstream, which is created by the propellers. Soon gravity takes over, and all you have learned in synthetic training comes into play. Jumping out of a plane is just a mean of transport. It's what you can do once you are on the grown.

CHAPTER 20

LEARNING TO FLY

When I say learning to fly, I do not for one moment want you to imagine I'm flapping my wings like Icarus. He flew under his own power, and well, but he had wings. When I was learning to fly, I was learning to navigate my parachute and keeping out of the others, a drill we learned. As gravity will insist, we pull down grown, so it's just a matter of maneuvering default to the ground. That is what I mean as learning to fly. Out of the plane, our kit is hooked on to out harness. When it's clear no one is near and nothing will endanger others, it is released. Sometimes it can and will oscillate; that has to be corrected before landing.

Today, you can see men flying in specially designed suits. I know I'm getting old when I must use words like "back in my day." We had just ordinary combat kit, ready for action when you hit the ground. Can a man fly, I'll say yes. The flight is not exceedingly long, but it prepares you, from the plane to your landing. Know where you are during the trip so you can steer the parachute to where you want to land. When you leave the airplane, you lay in the slipstream. For a few seconds it's joy, but it's soon over. Then you must check your place and others as you prepare to land. The important thing is that you land on your feet and then walk away fit with your kit. The kit may include such items as food, medication, and first aid, such as bandages.

Yes, they teach you to fly after you jump out of the airplane. The next is a flight assessment, carried out to make sure the parachute opens. Once that's completed, you had to look to see where you were in location to others, who were also doing the same jump.

You were told to look sideways to make sure you didn't cause someone to shoot because that would take the air away from you. You need to make sure your feet are in the right place and not over your head, and then as the ground is coming up close, you have got to get ready. Feet and knees and hands, chin on chest and arms in. Don't reach for the ground. It will come to you when you land. You had to break your fall by rolling over. That roll is feet first, and the rollover breaks the fall to stop the vibration from penetrating the spinal cord and sending you into unconsciousness.

Anyone can jump or be thrown out of an airplane, but you must first learn to fly, to ensure a safe landing, in most cases. After you have landed, that's when your test begins. Your physical fitness will come into play. You must be very fit and at the top of your game to pass at the school of parachutists.

At the RAF Station in Abington where they trained the parachutists, the school's objective is for you to jump out of an airplane and to walk away afterward. I was put through a series of synthetic training along with others who had already passed the course and come from various entry points. Jumping out is easy once you are trained, once you get over the fear of knowing you will be asked to jump. Synthetic training is crucial. It involves a series of running, jumping, and rolling. We were taught basic anatomy and physiology of the human body, about the nerves that run from the heel up to the brain and the spinal nerve center that keeps your balance. The aim is that when you get up after your fall, you know your left from right and which way to go. You must know the direction to go in because the drop zone is usually a wide-open plane, possibly a beach, jungle, or a desert. So during your training, you must know how to cope in all sorts of conditions. If it's windy, you could get dragged along, and your feet could get tangled while running to deflate and fold the parachute.

Parachuting is like a form of transport, although it doesn't take you all the way to your destination. A five-mile march often followed the landing in a full kit; that's when the fitness counted. We sometimes had to jump at night. This was all part of the course. My night jump took place over Salisbury Plain. We took off from Lasham military airport when we reached the Bristol channel. The jumpmaster was in contact with the pilot, and the pilot used to let him know when we were close to the drop zone. There would be a countdown in minutes. Then the jumpmaster asked you to clip yourself to the strong line. When it's your turn, you receive a tap on the shoulder and move forward to the open doorway. You feel frightened. The red light is on until the pilot tells the instructor, once, over the drop zone, the light turns green, and its time to jump.

Up in the air, we had to trust each other as checks were made for safety, and working as a team again was vital. So there was trust between one man and another. However, it was not so on the ground as prejudice existed. In the church, as far as I am concerned, an Anglican person spoke harsh words when he let out that blacks are beasts and have no rights or claims to God and should be eternally damned. Whatever gave him the right to be to a dog or was he just bluffing? Con men some of the clergies are, trying and succeeding at times to sell the rights to God.

If this kind of speech was what was bandied about in the sixteenth century, it's no wonder it wasn't taught in schools. I was never informed of slavery at school, nor of the colonizing of the small island. Let's look at the facts: the school textbooks were all written and printed in England, by Englishmen. Their instruction could well have been, not to mention slavery. It is a fact that for years there was a significant increase to the British economy, which came from the West Indies, mainly Barbados. This started in the 1600s and lasted until the 1960s. Sugar and cotton were the primary products, then later it was just sugar. Sugar was the backbone of the income, labor was needed, and Africa was the source, where a relaxed lifestyle was lived. Vastly different from the regimental way of residing in Europe, in Africa, men, women, and children wandered about half-naked, that is what the climate allowed. They had no fear or guilt about the body. They dressed to fit the environment only. This very nomadic way of life is still lived in parts of Africa today.

CHAPTER 21

I AM PROUD TO BE ONE

I am proud to be Bajan born and bred, not far from the capital St. Michael. For me, it was walking distance from my home. In the old language, we would say about a mile and a half.

That was where I went when I left school, where many people were busy working or trying to hustle a living. Many people held down two jobs as my aunt used to. For her, it was washing and ironing clothes, sweeping, cleaning, and cooking for those who were slightly better off and can afford to pay someone, maybe not regularly but temporarily. This would have been in the late 1940s, and I was approaching eight years old. Life was hard. I know that now, but I did not at the time because it was the same for everyone living in Carrington village. As I was growing up there, I was known as Florence's grandson, your parents and grandparents knew you. If you did something wrong, the news and the consequences would be awaiting you when you reached home, and it was that fast!

I am blessed funnily, not ha-ha, as you may believe, but I have managed to achieve a few of the goals that I had set for myself. I did not set my goals too high and then blame others for the lack of this or that. I am an immensely proud Bajan; you would have to go an awfully long way. Stack temptations in my direction to offer me things that I can't and wouldn't be able to afford. You could offer me a Rembrandt or a castle in the sky, but you couldn't take the island and its ways out of my life. Having said that, let it be known I'd fight for England and the UK if I was needed, without much persuading. I am a NCO (noncommissioned officer) trained rifleman, a qualified chef and paratrooper. Those are just a few of the strings to my bow. There are more, but they don't come easy. It is costly to train a man to become a paratrooper. Being in the army, I gained experience that could not be achieved anywhere else. No college or university tried to understand for years why I have not done things which are clearly quite popular with the public. Still, I could have supplied me with all I gain from my time in the army.

It was indeed a clear insight, as to glimmer a large number of people who are handled, housed, and held together and organized. Working toward the same outcome that benefits all, planning and pooling of the resources together, executing it, to make it work. As a young chef, I took part in one of the biggest NATO (North Atlantic Treaty Organization) military exercises of its time, on woodland ranges in Germany.

CHAPTER 22

THE FALLOUT OF NUCLEAR

There was no fallout. If there had been, I would not have been able to write the details of the plan for what it was. Not only that, I don't think the world could survive it. Life would be hell; we could become as zombies or as the living dead, feeding on whatever was left hanging around afterward, and the food would likely carry poison. Almost everything living thing on earth is contaminated. The water that feeds the plants, and subsequently, those plants would be unfit for food. They would become reduced in number, and if the bees go, we would be next. The bees are the pollinators, and we need the flowers to have fruit. Fruits multiply by the bees transferring the seeds and pollen from one to another. There are other animals that transfer seeds to grow, such things as birds transferred to fish, from one pond to another. They catch the eggs that are dropped into the water and so on and so on. That is life on earth as we know it, but I think a nuclear fallout would be just what it is—a fallout. I am not claiming to be a nuclear physicist. That I am not. I am requesting to be with human rights.

The year was 1962; the event is now known as the Cuban Missile Crisis. I was in the middle of a course to upgrade my skills at catering school in Aldershot. During those thirteen days that changed the world, yes, the world was never going to be the same after those tense, hot-wired days. When the world held its breath and prayed, we investigated the sky in readiness for a nuclear war. The dust has still been settling on the ground in Nagasaki and Hiroshima after being hit with an atomic bomb in 1945.

A turning point in my lifetime. It is said the genius that was Einstein warned; the men in suits ignore his warning: Don't use the weapon. It will be disastrous, they (the men in suits) ignored his words of wisdom, and it came to pass. It was as he told them, and it is still with us all these years later. I, along with others, was in the most prominent catering school in the world. We were learning how to bake a cake and roast a four rib of beef. At the school in the kitchen, the food we learned to prepare and cook was taken and served in the main dining room. What was not told at the time was that a nuclear winter would have followed, as the mushroom cloud would cover the sun for weeks maybe months. Nothing could have grown, and the temperature would have continued to drop. The dead would have remained unburied and all things that had once lived. One thing we were told was how to prepare food; however, food would not have been fit for consumption.

CHAPTER 23

NUCLEAR FALLOUT

I am nursing an extraordinarily strong belief that a nuclear war could shift the world off its axis. If you were alive when man landed on the moon, you could have experienced some enjoyment of man, getting there and back. The splashdown made world news as well as the launching.

Back in the 1960s, I think we were full of gloom. When the thought of nuclear war rose its ugly head, many said it was more than a thought, and the atomic weapons were being built and transported across the Atlantic. They already had satellites with a powerful lens and everything. When President Kennedy received the information that the Russians were sending nuclear weapons to the Caribbean, wow, it was game on. Makers of the bomb, the generals in their suits, had only one thing in mind, as far as I'm concerned, getting the weapons off the ground and into the air and fired when they wanted. Everything had to be calculated, including the distance the aircraft had to be when it went off because it would create such a vacuum.

That it might suck in that same aircraft that was going to drop the bomb. It had to be calculated and recalculated.

Another strategy that was being talked about was the phone lines between Washington and Moscow, were hotlines, to show they could be scorched. There was talk of war, and we were taken out of the kitchen and into the classroom. There we sat and listened to lectures of what might be had a nuclear bomb landed. No doubt London would have been a target along with Moscow and probably Washington. We were told in our lectures of what the aftermath of a blast would be like had we survived, and this was a tough conversation to have. President Kennedy said the communist leader had to turn his ships around or he would blow them out of the water! The world held its breath, and these were frightening words. I am pleased to say they came to nothing; just how much damage could have been done we will never know. The two men talked, and the conflict never happened.

Today, we are better informed about nuclear fallout. We have experienced the three-mile island accident at Chernobyl. Some of us have seen live on television the destructive action of a tsunami. The water leaves the shore and retreats far back only to come rushing in minutes later, destroying everything in its path. If you were walking on the beach and there was a nuclear explosion, I don't think you would stand much chance. Hiroshima and Nagasaki bear the marks of two atomic bombs.

On reflection, as I look back and recall those lectures, they were pointless. The lecturers were ignorant of the facts that we now know. A fallout feeds on oxygen, and that oxygen can cause suctions, as we know that fishermen, as far as seventy miles out to sea, suffered from the atomic bombs. Then there is the fallout where the animals would eat the grass and experience from different forms of poison. Yet some people and animals weathered the storm.

We were shown into a made-up bunker, and it was well stored with rations. We were taught what to look for and how to use it. We were shown a film about how the wind was used to feed oxygen to the blast, and the explosion would consume all the oxygen it could. Tiles were whipped from the rooves of houses and huts, one by one in quick succession, and trees would bend before breaking in one direction, the direction of the blessed. It is a frightening thought.

To my thinking, the world cannot afford a war of that type, of a nuclear blast. It's not so much the blast itself. It is the aftereffects that would last for years and years, leading to a shortage of clean drinking water and the inability to grow food. After the Chernobyl accident, the farmers' lambs and other grass-eating animals in Wales were suspected to be contaminated from the fallout.

The horrible day today, aftereffects would be disastrous for Mother Nature. The small insects like butterflies and worms that turn over the ground, and as for bees, flying with their tender wings, could they survive with Nintendo-structured wings. Could the birds survive? We have already made big mistakes, like when trying to get rid of a vermin infestation, and this can cause trouble to others. A similar thing happened some years ago when they tried to get rid of rabbits. The eagles fed on the poisoned rabbits. Something happened, and the eggs were not strong enough to bear the weight of the birds sitting on the nests; as a result, the eagle population went down.

What I am saying, whether you get it or not, is that we all rely on something else for survival, whether it is the food we eat or the water we drink. We can see this from when the US army sprayed crops in Vietnam from 1962 to 1971, for the dual purpose of exposing Vietnamese forces in the forest and contamination of the food supply to the enemy. It was called Agent Orange.

Where the bees go, we will follow, for we cannot fertilize. The bees do the pollination on their tiny little wings. It is unmeasurable the work that the bees do. On this course, they save us. Take that away from them, and we are starting to commit suicide. We the people must think about it. The rich, for some reason, believe they can get away to another place.

CHAPTER 23

WAR CAME CLOSE

They called it the Cold War: it was the heyday for spies, and there were lots of double-dealing. It was a time of mistrust between countries and their leaders. It was the aftermath of the Cuban Missile Crisis, and it had its peak from 1948 to 1953. However, the feelings ran on into the 1960s. The literature of that time tells its own stories; the cinema explained it in a way that only it could. At the same time, Britain was giving up on its empire, and it was too expensive to maintain and police.

The Europeans were making claims on other lands and people of that land. Were they not witnesses of the Second World War? Were they too blind to see what had just taken place—how people protected themselves from others who wanted their land and wanted to turn the people into slaves? Bulgaria, Hungary, and Czechoslovakia were all then under the USSR.

In the camp where I was a young soldier, just finishing my spell of square bashing, that is leaning in time with others, I learned the white fall in will come, giving time to obey the instructing.

I learned to march in time with the others in the squad. By now, I was at the catering school, where I learned to butcher and prepare cuts of meat and to position roll and tie joints. It was, to me, an individual school. Troops, came for lunch in large numbers. Men and women were trucked in from units nearby to be fed. We prepared, cooked, and served food for five to six hundred soldiers daily. It was very exciting. All ten of us had to take a turn at every part of the operation. It would be a show, other than from the school, just a course or two with be able what it looks like at that end of the course. To see how it all works from the preparation, one of the most crucial elements in cooking, be it a sweet-smelling cake for a surprise birthday cake, cocaine, or a wedding cake for numbers of any kind.

One must pay attention to all that it entails—baking, roasting, and serving. All of us took part in the management of catering, from stock-taking to ordering, menu planning, butchering, and all about seasonal fruit and vegetables. There was little use of frozen foods, as the market was in its infancy. We could only use what was available in the camp, and we had to learn how to deal with emergencies, such as the electric or gas supplies being cut off.

We were taken out of the kitchen and into the classroom. Day after day, we attended lectures on the fallout and what it would be like after the blast if we survived.

Let's face it. The world could not afford a nuclear war. We would all suffer after the explosions, one after another. If both went off, the sun would be blocked out. Without the sun, a cold would blow and oxygen levels would be incredibly low. So far, to date, there have been one hundred nuclear accidents, some more serious than others. We must be ready.

Nikita Khrushchev was a leader of Russia at the time. He played his card, and it brought us to the edge of World War Three. His aim was to put rockets in Cuba, and luckily, it was picked up by some smart guy by a ship coming down through the Atlantic. The large sheet of tarpaulin is made to be water-resistant, in navel color, but was not large enough to cover and camouflage all the rocket. He took pictures and got them to the notice of President John F. Kennedy. At that time, he got on the telephone and called the Russian leader with a threat.

CHAPTER 24

THE FOOD REVOLUTION

Changes in food, to be cooked and consumed in England, came in with the immigrants, in their luggage were recipes and the know-how in their heads. Handed down from mother's home, cooking, copying, and tasting of what was their food, back in the old country. Shipping brought in bananas, the sweet plantain, which is from the banana family and must be cooked. Lots of root vegetables appeared that had not been seen in the UK.

The airplane enabled a new variety of fish from the four corners of the world. Pulses also joined in on the act. The world of food, or is it food from around the world, had now been on sale in some parts of the UK. That started in the later fifties and early sixties. The staple diet of Africa and the Caribbean sprung up in the big cities. Fast food and takeaways came on the wings of the Chinese and both joined the English menu. Often when you looked at the menu list, a number went next to the dish, so you can callout the number. This stopped wrongfully pronouncing of Chinese dish, dim sum or egg foo young.

That was the dish you chose; it was known by its number name. Fish and chips were also classified as a takeaway. We have to thank the Jews for their input. The refugees brought that with them as they were kicked out from Spain and other parts of Europe. Europe's fast-food pizza is still one of the most popular takeaway dishes today.

French cuisine was well established along with the diplomatic language being French. In London, the menus were written in French—it was almost embarrassing at times. When the English diners had to ask, pointing out a dish on the list, the most common question asked was "What's in it? What is chateaubriand?" Today, many would reach for their phones and ask Google those questions, such as *daube* for example, which is Provençale of "beef."

In the 1960s, those who could afford it could go to French restaurants; however, few people could afford to eat out then, so it was a big deal, and they would dress up to go out for a meal.

Street cuisine soon followed, and London became a world food destination, with food from all over the world. The shipping routes were already in place as a result of bringing in the booty for the empire.

Shipping brought in the food. The docks were busy unloading whatever came into the empire. Transportation became a victim of itself; those in charge did not see what was coming. Something dramatic happened during those early years, leading to ships becoming obsolete, almost overnight. Containers would be the new way of shipping all products. The new technology must have seemed a dream, with refrigerated containers. The Clyde shipyard was building ships for the British to sail in, but something new was happening, and those in charge could not see the changes. The ferries had moved from vessels to containers, and that was one of the significant chain revolutions of shipping food across the world. We can all look back now and see where the shipyards went wrong. Just because you're big and powerful doesn't mean that it will always be so or that you will be able to keep up. The British ship industry died because it could not adapt. It was a slow death, after ruling much of the world for so long. The container industry cranked up and took over. This meant that the turnaround rate of a ship was hours instead of days. The whole shipyard would have to change. New hardware was needed to lift the containers off the boat and stack them. An old-fashioned crane was not up to the task.

They waited to be collected by lorries, which would take them to their final destination or the train, often just yards away from the dock, that took the goods and delivered them across the country. The juggernauts could do no wrong, with their bookings full. It was there for all to see, but those who needed to see did not. They continued to stick to what they knew.

With the influx of immigration started after the end of the Second World War, many, mainly from the empire, saw Britain as their home, a place of homage. Yes, there were many nationalities who, joined in the fight for freedom.

CHAPTER 25

A DREAM LIVED

I have lived some of my dreams, and now I am taking the time to share them with you. As I recall some of the good times, the bad I have locked away. Life for me was not easy at all. I wouldn't say I hold exclusive rights to that statement, for millions of others could say the same. It was challenging, and being dyslexic was added pressure I could well have done without when I was growing up. I developed a strategy to cope with it, and it has served me well.

When I think of the love I have had and lost, well, you feel the pain and the joy until it runs out; the pleasure lasted longer but some of it—the pain—is very hard to explain. It has driven some to kill each other. In France, crimes of passion have been carried out on someone loved. My interpretation is madness. Something happens inside us that drives us to kill. In my opinion, man has that built into him, to kill or to be killed, to survive. We can feel threatened—anything new seems to present a threat. In my story, you will read some of these things. It's probably no more than what others have experienced. I am not unique. I don't and never have expected any more than a fair share.

One time after I jumped off a bus, I felt something stuck in my ribs to threaten me, and for no other reason than the color of my skin, I was just standing at a bus stop. On reflection, it seems the perpetrators have a pack mentality. The big boy, who is more than likely shy, tries to show his skills in bullying and picking on a loner. To prove his worth in front of the group, he will attack, confident that his mates will back him should it not go his way. Take him aside from the others and stand up to him, and he will back down first. Had he known that I once wore the red beret and had it in me to kill, it might have been different, but without my uniform, I was just another black man. What could have happened had a fight started, and he had been arrested, and no knife or weapon was found on him? I could have been the one in trouble.

I think prejudices start at home. It could be at the table at mealtimes. It can also come from the church. I speak of the church because that is what I have grown up with in Barbados. The church I attended was like an upside-down boat with a wooden roof. It was consecrated in 1655. Britain and other European countries were heavily into the trend of buying and selling men and women. Yet, they were going to church every Sunday to pray for what they were about to receive. The Africans were forcibly removed from their homes and shipped across the seas. Seated and chained in the same seat for the duration of the journey, then to be sold then to be put to work in some of the most dangerous working conditions known to man. The island they were sent to would have been infested with a few unexpected provisions, like snakes that could hitch a ride on driftwood and find they could feed at sea as well as on freshwater.

At the end of slavery, the now ex-slaves were not allowed to worship in the church. We saw this in our time in the USA. In Barbados, they were not allowed in the church, so they gathered outside.

CHAPTER 26

THE COMPUTER AGE CAME

In the latter part of the 1940s and early 1950s, when I attended school, I often wished for a computer, not that I knew of the name "computer" or what it would look like. I didn't know what it would be called. I just wished for some help to navigate my schooling. I just wanted anything to help me. I had a strong feeling that something was out there, although it wasn't available at that time. It was just a dream in someone's subconscious. It was a dream of things to come.

Now let's look at the facts, the computer was always there in various scattered parts. The speedometer, for instance, is a type of computer. It can tell you how fast you are going, and at the end of the journey, it tells you how far you have travelled. The information recorded about the hundreds of miles travelled, recorded, and stashed away and saved for future reference. That is innocence it was computing. The computer, as we know, has a lot of components brought together in one housing. The keyboard came from the typewriter. There were already electronic clocks and voices could be recorded onto tapes and into text.

I applied for a Sinclair X 80, instead of a computer. I received a letter from the company, telling me that they were all sold out, and I could have my money back or wait until the X 81 hit the shelves. I opted to wait because there was no one else you could buy a computer from. As far as I was concerned, the X series was the first home computer. Yes, I was heading for a good home computer. The code breakers who worked for the British, they had computers, the first working computer then was in 1944 at Bletchley Park, and you can probably go back further. The computer itself is all about numbers. It brings with it slang terms like *bites* and *megabytes,* and mathematicians keep adding new words to the language of computing.

Today, I have a computer that masquerades as a watch. It works in conjunction with my phone. I get an alert vibration on my wrist that tells me my phone is ringing—that is, if I am close to my phone. This is also a warning to any potential killers who want to commit the crime of murdering someone. The act itself can be recorded in a slight hand movement. Somebody could be listening order messages being recorded by technology for you.

The computer is moving from a desktop to a laptop and to a mobile phone. This has all happened in a relatively short space of time. When you consider the latter, when the telephone was invented, it stayed in the house. It was given to the servants to answer; the owner did not want the intrusion. We are now wearing it, close to us and can get intruded on at any time of the day or night.

Once the computer age arrived, devices got smaller, and yet, they did the same job and replaced the larger models. Yet still, it is a fascinating time to be alive. I'm watching what can be done with these small machines and something called a chip.

The Computer Age Came

Not to be confused with a fried potato ready to eat. It is said that the disk is faster than the human brain in calculations and is now being programmed to think, to play chess and other card games. The latest version of the computer remembers, but it can't feel. That is technology at its best. At school, I longed for something to come along and help me with my spelling. I'm glad to say, it has arrived! I bought my first computer in 1981. It didn't do much. It was slow, but it was a forerunner for better machines that followed. I now wear a watch that not only tells me the time, but it records my heartbeat. It can also give me the weather report. When I was growing up, this kind of thing would have been like science fiction! My banking also can be done online. Whenever I need to, I can sit in front of my computer, as I do now, and pay my bills, look at my account, and arrange whatever needs to be arranged. It's convenient for me; however, it has led to some banks closing on the high streets, and people are becoming unemployed due to the technology in our everyday lives.

The computer can also be a thief. Some time ago, one of my bank cards touched my phone and I heard a little "bling" as I paid for something that I didn't want and didn't receive. That is technology. So much progress in such a short space of time can lead to confusion and errors.

You can pay for your coffee with a card, a bus ride, or a train ride, by swiping it or tapping in the four numbers that are unique to you. It is with us, and it's here to stay, for it has helped us in so many ways. But what happens if it falls apart or becomes corrupt beyond repair? We will have to go back to paper and lists and memos to ourselves.

The young men and women who got the computer up and running without laws or regulations ran amok. With every invention comes indentures, and the danger is the computer brought with speed and ease of use for some, such as the rigging of elections. The news spread and newspapers are on their deathbeds, critical and in need of a lifesaver. By the time the paper is printed and go on sale, it is all news to some who gets the news while it is actually happening. The phone is fast, small. It can capture photographs and send them down the line to the editor in the newspaper office.

The computer and the smartphone can spread the story swiftly, the papers as we know had an editor, and some items just did not get through to the general public. Now, today, we are all photographers, writers, and editors all in one. I find that weird. And that is news as we know it today. You could see a man being burned alive on television, doused in petrol or some other highly inflammable liquid. Someone strikes a match and up the flames go. By the time that the clothes are removed, the body would be severely burned and that can be seen live on television.

We could be in a mess, and the children would see it. There are no editors for such news. We are the consumers of the press; we are the makers of the story. Every one of us with a smartphone can film and upload it to the internet.

CHAPTER 27

THE COMPUTER CAME HOME

Making that big game-changer, first, it was a ball, travelling from side to side. That was fun, but it became tedious after a time. The speed of the computer gradually got faster as more RAM became available. Young men and women with higher education were in great demand. This was after a time of mass unemployment, a time when kids didn't want to go to school because their future looked bleak as they looked at their older brothers and sisters at home, under the door with no prospects in sight, until they were needed for this new venture.

Few people could see the potential of this machine. I could as far back as 1948. I wanted a device that would help me spell, as my spelling was so pathetic due to my dyslexia. I could not maintain the rhythm of the word and mental arithmetic eluded me. So I prayed for something like this to come along, and wow, it happened!

Like all new invention, it was rough to begin with, like the first motor car, which had to be cranked to start it. But it gradually got faster, slimmer, slicker, and lighter. Everything about it seemed so right. So much so that it's a watch on my right hand that can let me know when someone phones me. I can answer them on the watch, or I can then go to my mobile phone and see them as well as speak to them—the two are in tandem.

Along with the computer came computer crime, a new way of stealing money. Back in the day, you had a robbery carried out at gunpoint. In the 1940s after the war, there were a lot of guns around after the war, so that was a common crime—a way to get fast cash without much planning. As for the train robbery, that took a lot of planning, and it could still go wrong. If caught, then you would spend a long time locked up, and without money to live or a job, you would quickly revert to what you knew.

No one foresaw this, but then we could say that about the machine gun, being used by criminals for a quick killing.

What's fantastic is that you don't even have to be in the same country to commit the crime. Not in the same time zone nor speak the same language. The criminal just has to convince you that something is wrong and that your bank account has been compromised. They then say, "If you go to your bank and withdraw your money outside, there will be a security person who will take your money and deposit it safely in another bank." This trick has played out time and again, to the most vulnerable people. This is all new ingenious technology, those two wires. What allows us to speak to each other can now let others take all the money we earn away from us. If you have not been scammed yet, then you can count yourself lucky. The numbers are going up, of people who are being scammed, day after day.

The computer, whether you like it or not, is here to stay. It can be used to order goods, electronics, food, and a host of other products, and they will be delivered to your door, without you leaving your home.

CHAPTER 28

MEETING MY FATHER

I do not think a child should meet his father. It should be the other way round. That is part of my story. I had just crossed the Atlantic in a Boeing 747, pinned into my window seat by two large women sitting on my right. They were first-time travelers, visiting their relatives in England. I don't think I moved for the eight and a half hours sitting down the whole time. It was a night flight, so after dinner, I got my head down, and the next thing I knew, I arrived at Heathrow airport and went through customs and passport checks. Then I went down the stairs onto the underground to the Piccadilly line and got off at Manor Park. I hailed a taxi as I could not be bothered to hump my luggage on and off buses. I reached home, and the flat was empty. I was due to work the next day, so I settled as much as I could.

Then the telephone rang. I answered. A voice in my ears explained who he was and asked me to confirm my name. He then told me that my father was admitted to the hospital. He named the hospital. It was a popular East London one, and he gave me the details. I got up Monday morning and went to work, and then I went straight to the hospital after work to visit my father.

I asked at a reception after giving his name, and I was told which ward he was on. I made my way along there, asking directions as I went. Once on the department, after one or two turns, there he was. I had learned to recognize his face; it was not like my own at all. For nineteen years, I had not seen his face, yet it was imprinted from my childhood. We were two men when we met. I had to fight my own fights and make my own rules along the way and had gained a survival approach to life.

CHAPTER 29

MY FATHER'S DEATH

It was the morning I lost my father to death, and there was a phone call at about six thirty. This time, the voice asked me if I was Mr. Haywood's son. To avoid any confusion or explanation, I said yes. He then replied, "I am sorry to tell you that Mr. Haywood has died," and he gave me the time of death. By now, I was numb. A feeling had come over me; it was that of fear, naturally, for it was my first experience of losing a relative. I would be responsible for arranging the burial. It seemed like I was moving from a boy to a man overnight. Trust me, I had little idea how to arrange such things, but it was now down to me to do so. But now as I'm reflecting, I'm putting it so that others can read it, "as you sow, you will reap." He sowed the thought that nothing will touch me, or bother me, and yet now it was in my hands, and I would have to face the responsibility that I had not been groomed for.

Having two different names was one obstacle. I had to prove who I was. In those days, it was much more comfortable than now. I had to produce my passport and proof of my address. It could have been more of a problem if he had money, but he left no funds. I had to use my money, so that was one less thing to sort out. One of his brothers was called to the hospital before my father drew his final breath. So he stayed close and helped me to find directions to the funeral director and the undertaker. I had not been to a funeral in England, so I did not know what to expect. The morning of the funeral, we passed my father's address. It would be the last time he would give it and then all the entourage following behind the hearse with family and friends. I mentioned that he could have been cremated. Still, his ex-wife blocked me. She said something about burning in hell, so I arranged for burial instead of cremation.

I had been visiting Barbados for the past three weeks. While I was away, I tried to ring my father, but the phone just kept ringing for two days without success. It was then that I felt something could be wrong. Within an hour of being home in London, I had the phone call telling me that he was in the hospital and not doing very well. I was jet-lagged, so I visited him in the hospital the following morning.

His passing was not so much a painful loss for me. I had left Barbados nineteen years earlier and had lived in London for six years at the time. When I came to England, I joined the army, so we were much more strangers than father and son. I did not know him. I learned more of him through his friend.

So that left me with his flat, a flat so big that it could easily fit a family; I was living in it alone.

My father was not long in his grave, I lived in his three-bedroom flat. There were a few of his personal things there, so I left them on the fireplace. Sad to say that the builders who came in just helped themselves to his rings. I had sold the two diamond rings that he left me, maybe they went in the same way they came. As they say, easy come easy go. I was living alone and had to go to work every morning. Some work was being done to the outside of the building; some of the windows were replaced.

CHAPTER 30

A CHANCE MEETING

It was not long after my father's death in the late seventies. I had to pass quite a few pubs on my way to the French. It is on Dean Street, West London. In the heart of London theater land. You don't have to be a member, but it seems like that. The regulars stay faithful to the cause of conversation and drinking, with those who have time to kill and drink. This was in the days when Mr. Gaston Belmont was the licensee. I was drinking, minding my own business when an acquaintance came up and introduced me to an incredibly sexy young Indian-looking woman. I was a bit knocked back by her beauty up close. I had seen her on the other side of the bar (I could not help but notice such beauty), and she was everything one could think of as an Indian woman. Such smooth olive skin, the bone structure of her face was perfect. I looked at her eyes, and the bindi decoration was there between her eyes.

She wore tight-fitting blue jeans as some of the young Indian or Pakistan women had taken to wearing the western dress. They were so close that they hugged her skin, elastic woven into the denim. After a few drinks, I made a date to see her the next day for supper. On parting, I gave her my address and told her how to get there and station to get off, then bus or taxi to my place. I could not stop thinking about her on my way home.

The evening arrived; you could not have wished to meet a sexier young woman from that continent. Each country produces its very own brand of such beautiful women, none no more beautiful than the other. We talked. She was most charming with a very sexy smile. It seemed to show all of her teeth at the same time, but then I might have been dreaming for much of the time that I was in her company. While we ate, she told me that she lived in a palace, and I felt my pad left much to be desired. All these years later, it still may not be up to much, but to me, it's a bachelor's pad, with no net curtains blowing in the breeze and the feminine touch is missing.

She stayed the night, and before morning came, she showed me some of her acrobatic skills. When the morning did arrive, I had to get up and out, and she needed to get going as well. She asked me what time I would return, I ducked out of giving her an answer as I used to go to the pub most evenings.

The next evening, I came home later, and she was sitting on the landing waiting for me. The neighbor across the arrival had let her into the block. I don't know what she told my neighbor, but there she was. Security was not what it later became. On each of the six flats' doors was a letterbox; the postman used to have to walk up the stairs to deliver the mail. The postmen then would have needed to be very fit.

As she walked into my pad, I noticed a big red patch on the back of her dress. Her monthly menstrual period had started. So I ran around to the corner shop. Indian men run it. I knew the manager and asked him if he had some sanitary towels. He started to head down the aisle and then asked me what size. I did not think about that. Fool that I was, I thought one size fits all. He asked me if she was small, medium, or large. "Medium," I managed to reply. Once he picked it from the shelf, I paid for it and packed it and ran back to the flat. I asked her why she came, not knowing whether I would be in or not. It was then she told me that she came from a mental hospital. Well, you could have knocked me down with a feather. I must say to you that, at that point, the mobile phone was pure fiction, so I told her to get into the bath to get cleaned up and that afterward she would have to go back. I ran the hot water for her and told her it was ready. I made sure the water was the correct temperature. She closed the door and stepped into the bathtub. I could hear splashing and childish laughter coming from the bathroom.

While she was in the bath, I called the police, and they laughed at me. It may have been due to my choice of words when describing her. That could have been the reason for the outbursts of laughter I could hear down the line. I was cool about it and spoke in a low voice as the phone was close to the bathroom door. After the gaiety died down, they took my call seriously. They listened attentively, and I asked them to contact the hospital.

They made the call, and it turned out that she was one of their missing patients. I must say that I felt terrible, but I had to do it as there were no other options at the time. She then told me that the medication they were giving her was making her ill. After the bath, she got dressed (into the same clothes), and soon afterward, the doorbell rang. The police came in, including a female police officer. I still felt terrible that she had come to me for help; however, her problems were more than I could cope with at that time. My working schedule was a full one, often I would leave home at 07:15 a.m. for an 08:00 a.m. start, if there was an evening reception. It was my turn to work. After locking up, it could be well after 8:00 p.m. before I returned home.

CHAPTER 31

JAZZ A LANGUAGE OF LOVE

The language of America, jazz, arrived in chains. I thought I had completed everything that I wanted to say for the time being in this section of my life. But then, I remembered jazz. How could I leave without putting in a word about jazz? I have written on Facebook that jazz is the all-American language and it is!

Having crossed the wide Atlantic with chains on the hands and feet, sitting leg on each side of the seat, tightly chained to each other, chains passing through a loop that threated them together. That is how this American language arrived in America. These men and women carried it in their heads, the rhythm and the beat and the sound of the talking drum. That is how jazz arrived in America.

Coming from such an island that bathe daily mostly in the hot sun as Barbados, I can only imagine the way the slaves landed there when they arrived, in the same skimpy dress as when they were handcuffed. I sailed across the Atlantic from Bridgetown, Barbados, to Southampton in Hampshire, England. It was boring at times. For the class of ticket I had booked, I could walk around the decks, move where I wanted to move, and I was given the times when meals were served. But now I try to imagine what it would have been like having to sit from Africa to Barbados. Bodily functions carried out in the same place where you were chained to others both for men and women. For that journey across the Atlantic Ocean, it must have been harrowing and doesn't bear imagining what it was like on that slave ship.

I know the nights get very cold on the Atlantic. When I first felt the cold winds, I took to my allotted cabin and sat and pondered the experience. Although I had a blanket to keep me warm when I needed it, I still felt the cold biting into my body, the first time I felt cold.

If we reverse the obvious and imagine it was the Africans who kidnapped people from America and took them to Africa, I am sure they would not have lasted. Their resilience does not parallel that of the Africans. I think this illustrates how badly they were treated. It is sometimes good to put yourself in the shoes of another to get a feeling of how you may react, if put in that situation.

These men and women were seconded, half naked with marks from the rope burns, cuts on their feet, gaping wounds showing the early stages of gangrene. The only medicine available was saltwater, dragged up in a bucket by one of the trusted deckhands. One of the duties of a deckhand was to wash away human waste from the decks. With the hot sun beating down on them, the stench would have been unbearable. It proves that the human body can cope with a lot in the struggle for existence. Being fed just the bare necessities to keep them alive until they reached land and were put up for sale, the slaves were usually given one meal a day if at all, and it was likely gruel while the crew and deckhands were fed on beans, corn, and rice with palm oil.

Records show that the prisoners were very tightly packed, and they could not move to relieve themselves. We can only imagine the strangers they were sitting next to. From those who were onboard, we know that fresh water was limited. So there they were, chained to their seats without freedom to move for the duration of the journey.

Recall that during the Second World War, the body again was pushed to the limits of survival for some. People were worked to death and yet it was no stranger to them. It could come at any time, often while working. This same method applied in the concentration camps and this was during my lifetime.

Some of the languages that were brought in with the immigrants were English, Spanish, German, Yiddish, Greek, and Swedish—all arriving with their languages memorized and being used by them as they sought a better life in America.

The black men and women who arrived in chains had no passport, no stamp or number as many of the immigrants mentioned above would have been given.

Jazz was brought into America as the new language; the facts speak for themselves. Jazz was not in Africa, nor was it anywhere else in the world. It must have been inside, for the bearers of this new music, had it in their heads. So many of them we can trace, playing instruments, yet they did not own sheet music; therefore, new written words would be added to the American diction.

Jazz was new and anything new has all the difficulties establishing itself as well as fighting off its critics and nonbelievers. The law closed them down, often misunderstanding what was going on. A license would be required, for premises, licensed for selling bootleg whiskey. For its patrons, you could only enjoy the music if you purchased a meal. The new laws were written and designed to keep the black men and women in their place. That is anything that was a threat to the establishment. Jazz, with its syncopated rhythms, sent a message to parts of the body, causing it to start gyrating. There was hand clapping, foot tapping, which set the people to move in a fast and furious fashion. Head and feet, hips and the whole body moving in unison, it was new, and the dancing that came with it was very energetic and erotic. The bootleg whiskey, along with the music and dancing, sent messages to the brain and the male hormones, which naturally started to seek outlets.

Africa is known for its drumming. Whether it was done on starched animal skins or a hollowed-out tree trunk, drumming is what the Africans are known for. Some are called talking drums, and it can be used as a form of communication, probably like the North American Indians, communicating and spreading the news to the nearby villages.

Jazz is strictly American, make no mistake. It followed the blues, the telling of the hardship of working the fields, day in and day out, under the hot sunshine.

Jazz was in its infancy. Men in suits, why rejected it? Because it was new and anything new had to earn its place. Segregation also got in its pathway; some black men and women were not allowed in white-only venues. Yet it was taking hold on the community of blacks only. It was downbeat, and it was wild; it was raw, as it was meant to be. It rode piggyback on the blues and told about love and loss—life portrayed in short stories. They had to make their way into and out of love, the courtship of life in Africa, taken from other formats of music. Still, the men and women who sang, strummed, or beat on the drums continued this genre of music. Tap dancing hooked a ride on the rhythm of the pulsating jazz. From the way of administrating the law was copied and accepted. Anything new found it much harder to be accepted. Jazz fitted that category. It was new, and the innovators were blacks, who could not register to vote. The term was not in use then but fitted into the same vein as "nonpeople," which was used. You had the right to disagree, but looking at the facts, you will see why I made my claim that jazz is American, and it is the American language.

Jazz was not in Africa, nor was it in America, nor was it made anywhere along the Atlantic coastline. Those men and women who were being trafficked from one continent to another had it in them. No, not at all. It would have stemmed from being bound and chained, deprived of freedom, that would make them look for an outlet for their feelings. Had slavery not happened, we may never have seen the foot-tapping, hip-jogging, and waist-twisting that united them to this new language. After all, they did not know each other, did not all speak the same language. You have to imagine the picture when the slaves arrived on the boats; they had nothing other than the clothes they stood up in. Some of them may have been set to work the same day they arrived. All the surroundings being strange to them, compared to what they had left in Africa.

They were put to work nearby not knowing each other, not speaking the same language of their coworkers or their captors. They had to listen and not talk back. That must have been exceedingly difficult. They survived against the odds!

Today, the stories are coming fast and furious of the experiences that men and women lived through—those harsh and brutal days when Americans, Spanish, Portuguese, and other Europeans took what they wanted. Africans were chosen purely for labor, unpaid, of course, and starved and used in America and the Caribbean.

No other Americans, living or dead, was so severely treated the way the African Americans were. From day one, they had no access to any of the rights that other Americans enjoyed. American residency was also denied and their right to live where they wanted. Voting was not permitted for them until 1924 when Congress granted that right, so any laws written before that date excluded them. It still did not happen as it was meant to when everyone was allowed the right to vote, because, not everyone obeyed the law, therefore in some states, it was not enforced.

Some rules have lain dormant and are still used today. England, some were written in England for the English, can even be used in Barbados as they were in the days of slavery. Dreams from their homeland, that was the rhythm of the men who gave us the language of jazz. Sadly, the men and women were in chains when the concept was born.

The giants of jazz are the big names we all know. Scott Joplin was known for piano rags; he learned some classical music from a German immigrant. Joplin's work included *The Entertainer*. They made history with their music and their playing and their dress. The dress was as outrageous as the music, if not more so. They imitated European evening dress, and black musicians wore morning dress, borrowed from the way the Europeans dressed. Then the 1930s brought a new style of clothing to suit the dancing. The craze then swept across the USA.

It was lovely to listen to, as they played it so enthusiastically with real meaning. And the way it was played was with foot tapping, a steady repeated rhythm, over and over, in time and out of time, that is jazz. No one person can rightly claim that he or she invented it. Like it or not, it was first played and listened to in America by black men and women, the offspring of slaves.

Only some knowledge of the people knew it and understood it. Others refused point-blank because they did not understand it. It followed alongside the blues, and they evolved side by side like cousins. The blues explained the hardship of working and living, the pain being borne, day in and day out, from sunrise to sunset. Most of the singing resulted from the "hoof" of being out in the fields and working in the hot sun fields from sunrise to sunset. They were not allowed to speak to each other, and they came from different tribes, so they spoke different languages anyway. It was a language born out of bondage, suppression, and segregation by black men and women who worked and paid tax but had absolutely no say where their money was spent.

In the 1800s, music was being played in West Africa, but it was not jazz as we have come to know and love it, as some of us do. In Africa, it was known as talking drums. That's not jazz, which is strictly American, make no mistake.

It travelled across the states. The airwaves that carried it were hot. To some it came naturally. It was like wildfire; it took roots in more than those who rejected it. Anything new is more likely to be rejected, often out of fear and ignorance. What people don't know, they instinctively jumped to hit the reject button. The new Americans and the Germans both rejected jazz during World War Two. I would say probably for the same reason aforementioned, that which is not understood is rejected out of fear.

The haunting song "Stormy Weather" was written by Harold Arlen and Ted Koehler and was sung by Lena Horn, first recorded by Ethel Waters in 1933. This for me defines the blues. It's about love and a love that was lost, a sad reminder of the one that got away. The Wall Street crash of four hard years was having an effect on everyone. The poor men and women felt it more, black and white. The bump and grind that had been lived out every night in the dimly lit nightclubs that sold bootleg whiskey was a relief for some.

Jazzmen and women who later became legends were often hounded by the police for taking drugs and any other charges the police could lay on them. Those that made it to the recording studios have left their work for us. Some of it in boxes, stored and locked up. It is difficult for some of us today to imagine what life was like, living in a segregated country, when everything was against you. The law was stacked against them, written mostly men who could not understand the pain. The housing was inadequate and often overcrowded. Education in most states was allowed more money per head for white children than black children.

Washrooms, bars, and public conveniences were all segregated. When I was growing up in Barbados, something similar was in place. Every working man and woman all had to pay their taxes. It got so bad that the police started planting drugs in bathrooms, just to make a charge.

Most of the jazzmen and women scratched a living, often living in inadequate accommodation. I have been fortunate enough to have seen a few of them. I saw Ella Fitzgerald at the Royal Albert Hall in 1984, and I sat just above her when she performed one of the songs by the Beatles, "Money Can't Buy Me Love."

When on tour in the USA, they had to stay on the touring bus as they were not permitted to book into a hotel. Despite the obstacle of segregation, the work and art they managed to produce are what I am willing to call American language. The black men and women were told to move along, continually being harassed by the police enforcing the law.

Miles Davis, the celebrated jazz trumpeter, stepped outside the recording studio and was beaten by a policeman, just for standing to smoke a cigarette and seeing a friend into a taxi. Racial prejudice is extremely negative thinking, yet it spreads and engulfs those in its web.

Black men and women fought in two world wars, three if you count the civil war. They fought in the name of freedom; to some, it might have seemed that freedom would never come. We'll never get there if we go on fighting for something that seems so elusive. They were not respected, not preheated for the work they did, in teeming the land—planting, weeding, and watering and then harvesting what the earth produces. The pain was the constant day in day out.

They came to Europe and fought for freedom, and some gave their lives in the quest for democracy. The liberation they fought for was not their own.

Jazz also was a prisoner along with its creators. No charge or crime committed, yet it was locked away from the people. History seems to have granted very few of them prosperity by recording their names. They have become rubbish in the dustbins of history, not on the pages of the storybooks that tell of history. In this case, history seems to hold in higher respect the victors than it does the so-called victims. Dominion over others is like beauty—it's on loan, you have it today, and the next day it's gone.

There are numerous names in jazz, and a few are Morton, Armstrong, Bechet, Brubeck, and Monk. I could go on, for the list is so long, all those who made it and followed their dreams. Women also endured all the hardships of singing and playing jazz. Ella Fitzgerald introduced her part of the language; it is called scat singing.

Other cities across the world came to love and understand jazz; in France, they called it "le jazz." In Germany, soldiers at night tuned into the USA forces network to hear it. The music with its beat was so new to some that they were bowled over by it. Word got back to Himmler, and he banned it, calling it degenerate nigger music. In 1935, a law was passed by the Nazi government; other musicians were also forbidden from imitating the jazz players. In hindsight, they should have banned themselves when a few of them tried and failed miserably to execute their leader.

Had the American generals taken a little time to learn, in my opinion, it could have ended the war sooner, by at least two years or more. They missed all this because segregation would have stopped them from learning. It is my opinion; jazz could have sent signals and messages to other parts of the forces. After all, it has been done before, during the times of slavery, hymns were sung that had meaning for those who wanted to hear it. There is a claim that on the underground trains, messages and codes were in them, but you had to know of them and listen out for them. To translate and tell others, such as when the train was leaving, you simply had to be ready. It's sometimes the case that everybody has something to offer, not just the person doing one specific job, but to listen to others and ask for their input. The mistake of the early Americans was made that way, and they thought because you were a slave, you, therefore, had no sense, nothing to offer. You were just a slave, and that was it! Get back.

Today, jazz has been taught in schools, across the USA and in other parts of the world, to all those who want to learn. How to play it and add their own interpositions, why? Because there was none before. The arts are for all, and they're there for everyone to learn, to play, or to dance to, because jazz is fun.

As was around me when I was young, it was purely African music, but then I wasn't in uniform. You had to know where to come in and where to get off.

Today some experts can analyze the music, the rhythm, the syncopation, and the meaning of it, but do they know? No one can ever know the hardships that gave birth to this music. Jazz was in their heads when crossing the Atlantic stemming from all they had withstood and the emotions this evoked. They had no instruments, no clothing, no rules, other than that of survival, and that's where jazz came in—through survival.

During the siege of Malta, the people were starving—no food, no fuel, and low on ammunition. All they had was hope. The German fighter pilots severely damaged the SS *Ohio*. The captain gave orders for it to be scuttled and asked the men for suggestions. The seamen and crew came up with "let's try and keep the two ships together and keep the old ship afloat." The captain agreed, and the crew put their idea to work. The ship limped into the harbor with all or most of its oil, for the people of Malta. I say, break up the exercise or objective and listen to the people. One of them will know or think of something that you don't! That is the art of positive thinking.

CHAPTER 32

SUGAR AND THE ECONOMY

I don't know why the Englishmen started Atlantic slavery. It puzzles me as to why they took to sailing to Africa and stealing men and women who had done them no wrong. Sugar then was the equivalent to gold in later years. Europe went crazy for it and developed a sweet tooth in every mouth across various countries. Sugar is now in the "dock" as it is seen as unhealthy for people. Here in England, you will find sugar in almost everything. It once was probably seen as a health stimulant, when, in fact, sugar just gives energy to the body. It comes from various plants, and sunlight turns it into energy. Sugarcane and sunlight together produce carbohydrates, which is the fuel that runs our bodies. You can also get carbohydrates from various other plants that receive sunlight, and sugar is one hundred percent sugar and no fats. The body manufactures it for quick access to action, which is usually known as fight or flight. If you cannot fight, you may be better to take flight and run. However, if you don't use the sugar, the body has an unwritten contract where it stores the energy in case it's needed for later.

So imagine that you continue taking in the same diet, including sugar, and it doesn't get used up. It turns to fat, so then you get overweight people unable to walk in some cases, and even the undertakers are reporting that the coffins are too small.

Today, sugar is in the "dock." It's the bad boy of health, getting blamed for fat children, for making children run amok with hyperactivity, and making adults obese.

Let's go way back to 1700, and this was the gold of its time. It had the same effects as gold had on men. It became a rush to get the land ready for planting sugar, and sugar was priceless in Europe. In almost everything we read, we learn that exercise is needed to keep a healthy weight. Therein lies the problem, when people watch television, play computer games, and have the wrong diet, it will lead to weight gain. In sugar's defense, used in moderation as part of a balanced diet and a healthy lifestyle, it will not cause these problems.

Nobody knows just how many men and women were forcefully taken from Africa to work in the production of sugarcane and cotton. The land had to be flattened and made ready to plant. A lot of attempts were made, and a lot of them failed. Some slaves and some slave masters went mad from sunstroke, and others went broke. Yet loads of men took the chance and sailed to the islands in the hope of making production and profit. Men in high places were made rich by supplying ships and crew. The top tables in the land sat to eat and drink from their earnings—Humphrey and Maurice bank managers in the city of London.

The rape of Africa took its revenge on the rapist. A sort of cancer spread, and it started with one man. I mentioned him earlier for his part in the start of the slave trade. He may have seen that Arabs and their camels trailed across the desert, for it is known that some African kings traded men and women into slavery as early as 1600.

As I say, just because you see others doing something terrible, that doesn't make it right for you to do the same. The scenarios that came from the war, when food was hard to get, often brought out the worst in people. They had to stand in line, hoping there would be something to buy, at a butcher's shop, for example. You had to stand in the queue waiting for the doors to open. You don't know what you are queuing for, but just hoping there will be food or meat your family need. It's in human nature. In that pack environment, survival is essential.

As I was out one evening, I saw a man after a disturbance, and I saw the windows were smashed and some low-priced jewelry was glittering in the window. I stayed, enduring the commotion and watched the police with their loud police sirens and all of the disruption. The next morning after it had boiled down, the crowd had moved on. I decided to go for a walk to see the damage. Few others were also out walking looking at the cost. There was a burned rubber still smoking, a man who was with his boy son. He just left the child on the sidewalk and stepped through one of the broken windows and picked up one or two watches. He looked at the first one and put it by, picked up another one and put it down and stepped back out through the broken window. I was left standing by his boy, and then they just continued walking. Nothing happened, but what he was doing was planting a seed in the child's mind, that as long as the door or window was open, you could just help yourself. That probably would come back to memory; some of the experiences would lie dormant in the child's mind, and only sprout into action when the chance arises. How sad that is, to know the father should be sealing the child's subconscious.

CHAPTER 33

HUNTE ON JURY SERVICE

I was selected for jury service in July 2010. There are no exemptions or schoolboy excuses accepted. Everyone on the register to vote is entitled to serve on the jury. I see it as an honor to help my peers. To be honest, I thought it had bypassed me as I had just reached sixty-five years. There is a cut-off line for your time. If your time has reached its end, you are no longer required for this service. Once selected you to have to report to the court on the day stated in the invitation letter that you receive by post. Within that letter are a lot of dos and don'ts.

It was an inconvenient time for me, as I was being treated for prostate cancer, but to my relief, the cancer is not active. I had all the symptoms, like getting up five times a night to pass water. Whenever I was out and about, I was always looking for the nearest toilet.

After the treatment, I no longer needed to run to the gents to relieve myself. Previously, I often consumed large amounts of liquid, and I liked standing in the pubs and drinking. At that time, it was whiskey and water, a bit too much of both. This was usually right after I finished work. I also had plantar fasciitis, policeman's foot to you and me. My hospital appointment was to be on the first day of my jury service and it was most inconvenient.

I turned up on the first day at the Crown Court along with a few other men and women. The building was heavily guarded. To enter the holding room, one must pass through an airport-type security. Bags were searched, and the body was scanned before entering the room. A pass was handed to me, containing my name and the extraordinary general information on a little plastic ID card. This had to be handed back at the end of my service. I strongly think it's an honor to serve on the jury.

If you are selected, it lets you see into the lives of others and experience, which one would never know unless they took on this service. For the other jurors and I, we met for the first time, and we waited while the coordinator told us what was and was not expected of us. We sat around reading newspapers and magazines, watched television, and waited to be called through. As I looked around the room, there were various lists. One that caught my eye was the number of religions there are. If you are Christian, you swear on the Bible. If you are Muslim, you swear on the Koran, or if you are Jewish, you take your book or whatever you use for your teaching. All religions and nonreligious were accounted for, and there was a list of what you should say when taking the oath or whatever represents your religion.

This went on for three days before I was called. It was the same routine every morning: when you got there, you punched in and then sat around waiting and waiting. It's an extraordinary duty to perform, and you are called upon because you are under the voting list.

One evening when I got home, I was welcomed with a letter from the hospital, so the next morning, I took the message and explained it to the coordinator. She told me to write a short note, which an orderly would hand to the judge, and this allowed me to explain the situation to the judge.

For my appointment at the hospital, I had biopsy samples taken, and I went home to bed afterward to sleep off the anesthetic. As I lay in bed, recovering from the anesthetic, my doorbell rang, and there was urgent knocking. I managed to pull myself up and crawl to the door. One of my neighbors from downstairs was concerned about the smell of gas in the house. It was like a dream sequence to me as I was in pain that this was happening.

He had already called a plumber. When the plumber came, I was trying to find the source of the smell. It seemed to come from my bathroom as I had a geezer in there at the time, though it could have come up through the floorboards. Whether he resolved it or not, I do not know, for I took to my bed. Then he called and asked for his payment—cash was his preference—so I had to go to the cashpoint and get him his money.

The night came and went, and I continued my jury service the next day. I was selected for the jury service and later summoned to serve on a jury—the case of some young teenagers who had stolen another's bicycle. The incident lasted for one day. We reached the verdict, and it was passed that there were no convictions. The experience I gained from being a juror was priceless, as I got to see how the system works. In civilian life, it is much different from how it works in military life, and there is no jury in the armed forces.

CHAPTER 34

AN INVITATION TO AN IMAGINARY MEETING

Here are some of the people who have lived that I would love to meet and know more about. So if I could, I'd loved to invite them to a dinner party. The invitations would go out, and I would gather them in a room for an informal powwow, where everything and anything could be talked about.

I have been overly impressed by some of the work that these men and women have done in their time here on earth.

Most of them were severely badly treated, like Nelson Mandela, Mahatma Gandhi, and Jesus Christ. Dorothy Dandridge suffered racial discrimination around Hollywood when she was an actress. She put in a particularly good performance in the 1957 film *Island in the Sun*. The film itself could not be shot in America due to racial problems.

Michael Hunte

MY IMAGINARY DINNER PARTY GUESTS

NELSON MANDELA. He served twenty-seven years in prison, just for wanting the right to vote. He walked out of jail with a smile on his face. At that time, he was the longest man to be held in captivity. Sometimes I ask myself what good did it do, to vote in his country?

DOROTHY DANDRIDGE. A Hollywood actress who left us too soon. I think she had a lot more to offer, but she took her talents with her. I remember her for her work in the film *Island in the Sun*. It was a movie of its time. It was written in America but shot in another country. There was segregation in America at the time. A kiss between a black actor and a white actress caused uneasiness in America.

MAHATMA GANDHI. He took on the British, which was a challenge because it's a big army, and he was facing political incompetency. He stood tall in his loincloth; he spun the cotton on his spinning wheel that made the cloth. He stood up to the might of the British army with guns pointing at him. He was beaten and arrested for his right to vote.

ALEXANDRE DUMAS. A master of his time, he was an official in the French army under the leadership of Napoleon. He wrote books and is famous for writing *The Three Musketeers*. He also wrote cookbooks. However, after his death, he was buried in a pauper's grave. It was a genius move by the then French president Monsieur President Chirac, and he gave orders for the body's remains to be exhumed and rebuked. He now lies in the Pantheon in Paris, France.

An Invitation to an Imaginary Meeting

ELLA FITZGERALD. I first saw her on a Saturday morning at the movies. Later, I got to see her at the Albert Hall in London, and she sang "Money Can't Buy Me Love" by Lennon and McCartney. She had a way of interpreting the language of jazz.

JESUS CHRIST. The son of God. Quite a lot has been written about the son of God. I cannot write about him, but I would love to meet him. Then I would get his thinking about the state of play today.

WILLIAM SHAKESPEARE. What can one say about the great author that hasn't already been said? Happy homage to his grave in the church in Stratford England. His work shaped a lot of the English language as we know it today. That man had a future, and he saw it, that his work would live on. Most of us use Shakespeare's words in our daily use of the English language. The house where he was born is still standing.

MILES DAVIS. I'd like to ask him a few questions. One especially important question was about himself and Bill Evans when they met for the first time in segregated America. They had something special, and it was in their work *Sketches of Spain*. Listen to that record and think yourself lucky to be able to hear, a man and his music. What a legacy he left us to enjoy long after he had departed from this life. When a genius is forced to leave his country, you know something is not right with that country.

ANGELA DAVIS. If we were the only two people alive, it would be nice to ask Angela a few questions. Just because you are dead, doesn't mean that your work must die with you, for she is definitely a woman of our time.

MARILYN MONROE. I strongly think Marilyn was a fine talented actress and singer. She studied at the Actors' Studio under Lee Strasberg in New York, along with some of the most influential actors and actresses of the twentieth century. I would have a conversation with her, asking an explanation for almost everything that has been said, to get a full rounded out picture. The work they captured on film was not digital, and that quality can still be seen. If you look at her job now, there's a good chance that you'll see something that you missed when you saw it at the cinema, especially as we have instant replay now, which was unheard of then. Now you can playback time and again until you pick up the story. Her work with Jane Russell in the film *Gentlemen Prefer Blondes* was released in 1953.

The End

www.ingramcontent.com/pod-product-compliance
Lightning Source LLC
Chambersburg PA
CBHW070912080526
44589CB00013B/1268